# TUTU
# THIN

*A Guide to Dancing Without an Eating Disorder*

# TUTU THIN

**Dawn Smith-Theodore**, MA, MFT, CEDS

*TuTu Publications*

ISBN: 978-0-578-15673-6

Published in the United States by TuTu Publications, Calabasas

This book is dedicated to dancers who may be struggling with an eating disorder, may know someone who has an eating disorder, or to someone who wants to be a dancer and wants to know how to prevent the development of an eating disorder.

This book is also dedicated to the memory of my mother, Nellie Lou "Skipper" Downie Smith, who introduced and taught me how to dance.

# CONTENTS

# FOREWORD

T IS DIFFICULT to understand the mindset of a person with an eating disorder and even harder to grasp how that mindset can overtake someone who needs a strong healthy body to participate in an activity they love, such as dance. It's well known that within the population of ballerinas there is an unusually high incidence of eating disorders. Being thin has been promoted (and even been mandatory in some cases) for ballerinas for quite some time now. But starving such that one can't dance is not supposed to be part of the equation. What's more, eating and purging food in order to avoid weight gain is also commonly seen in dancers and often results in serious psychological and physical consequences. All of this is very difficult for loved ones, teachers and friends to comprehend. At the same time, we know there are complex reasons why dancers might be more vulnerable to eating disorders. Traits such as perfectionism, make good dancers and with the right circumstances, breed eating disorders. Dawn Theodore is in a perfect position to understand and explain the complex chain of events that turn diets into disorders in dancers. She grew up in the dance world, developed an eating disorder and recovered from the disorder. As a dance teacher and psychotherapist, she has subsequently dedicated her career to dancers and people with eating disorders, particularly those individuals who happen to be involved with both.

In her book, *TuTu Thin*, Dawn tackles the topic of eating disorders in the dance world in a way that has not been handled to date. She helps dance teachers, parents and dancers understand how an eating disorder can take over and how to prevent the kind of thinking and behavior that will lead to a serious problem. She offers advice on what to look for and how to address a problem when it arises. Dawn's extensive training and personal experience lend the book credibility that only someone who has "been there and done that" can give. The book also offers several case examples of dancers, which helps personalize the information and make it more engaging. Readers will get specific advice and information on finding the balance between life and dance, nutrition tips and even treatment options when things have gone to a level where professional help or guidance is needed. *TuTu Thin* is an important addition to the eating disorder field as well as an essential book for anyone in the world of dance.

Carolyn Costin, MA, MEd, MFT, CEDS
*Chief Clinical Officer, Monte Nido & Affiliates*

AUTHOR:
*Your Dieting Daughter*
*The Eating Disorder Sourcebook*
*8 Keys to Recovery From an Eating Disorder*

# PREFACE

GREW UP IN front of a mirror. We lived above my mom's business, a dance studio. When I was eight, my parents built the red brick building that had two studios on the first floor. The house was the only one with a business on the street lined with Cape Cod-style homes. There was a circular driveway with a parking lot in the back, a drop-off spot for the dance students who would arrive after school, and on Saturdays. Every day after school, I would walk down the stairs to the dance studio where I was either in dance class, or working at the reception desk. I spent most of my free time dancing or working in the studio from the time I was three years old.

I was a thin child who could eat whatever I wanted. I modeled as a small girl and young teen and I remember seeing the famous, waif-like model Twiggy at a local department store in Cincinnati when I was ten years old. My mom and I made the thirty-minute drive to downtown Cincinnati to see the '60s icon at a local department store. She was doing a promotional tour and Ohio was one of her many stops.

I'll never forget her eyes the minute she walked on the runway. They were captivating, large with long lashes, some painted on for an exaggerated look. Her body was thin with no curves, and with her stylish haircut, she resembled a young boy with big eyes. I myself had no curves. When I began to develop and my weight crept over the 100-pound marker on the scale, I felt uncomfortable. It meant leaving my "Twiggy" body behind, an image I held up for myself for many years.

As a teenager, I longed for the body I had as a child. I had loved that thin figure as I moved across the dance floor in a leotard. My stomach and breasts were flat as a dancer's body should be. The optimum words to describe my childhood body were "should be." But who had determined this ideal body type for a dancer? It was me. I was listening to the drill sergeant in my head, to the voice that never stopped shouting and proclaiming that I wasn't good enough and needed to lose weight.

Lose weight I did. When I was fifteen, I was on a cruise in the Bahamas and spent too much time lying in the sun. I got sick from severe sunburn and lost a few pounds by the time I returned home. It was those few pounds that kicked the competition with myself into gear. If I lost five pounds, then how much better would I look if I lost another five pounds? This competitive game took over my thoughts. I spent hours planning my caloric intake for the next day. I began to cut foods that I had always enjoyed out of my diet. Rules began to develop that helped structure my life. For example, I wasn't allowed to eat or drink past 2:30 in the afternoon. I needed to make sure that all the calories I consumed during the day were burned off before I went to bed. This was the beginning of the war between my eating disorder and the small part of me that wanted to be healthy, to dance and explore the world.

During my illness, which began in 1972, there were unfortunately, no treatment centers dedicated exclusively to eating disorders. Very few people even knew that I was suffering from a mental disorder called anorexia nervosa, which turned out to have the highest mortality rate of any psychological disorder. I was tormented with thoughts of food, exercise and calories all day long. I carried a calorie counter book with me everywhere because I wanted to be sure I never went above the allotted amount of calories for the day. I continued to dance every day so the input did not equal the output. I continued to lose weight until my family recognized that there was a problem.

Starting at the age of sixteen, my mother took me to see my family physician every week to be weighed. He was a kind doctor, slightly balding with soft brown eyes, but other than putting me on a scale, he was unsure of what to do. His office was small and crowded with patients waiting to be seen. I always remember the terror of going there with the anticipation of what my weight had done or if something was medically wrong with me. Standing on the metal contraption in the hall was traumatizing, the number could never be low enough.

The doctor diagnosed me with anorexia nervosa, but admitted that he wasn't sure how to treat me. The idea of sending me to a therapist or dietician was not even an option we explored. Looking back, I realize I should have been hospitalized or at least admitted to a residential treatment center, if one had been available at the time.

With lack of direction, my journey to health was a long one filled with peaks and valleys. I still visited my doctor's office weekly to be weighed, and also have labs to make sure that I was medically stable. Yet, I was eating fewer calories, while continuing to dance every day. At the same time, my weight was becoming dangerously low and I wasn't getting my menstrual cycle.

Over the next few years, my weight fluctuated with periods of time when I would be at a healthier weight. I wanted to dance and gaining enough weight to have energy was an incentive, but I was still suffering.

When I was seventeen, I auditioned for the Rockettes as a summer replacement job. I'd wanted to be a Rockette from my very first visit to Radio City Music Hall when I was six years old. I loved to watch the precision of the dancers, their high kicks and beautiful costumes. It became a tradition to attend a Rockettes performance every time my mother and I were in New York.

When the day came, I couldn't believe that I was actually auditioning for the Rockettes. I checked myself into the stage door and took the elevator up to the rehearsal hall where there were many dancers stretching and warming up in preparation. The first part of the audition was to stand against a measuring stick to see if I met the height requirement at the time, which was 5'5 1/2". Well, I was 5'4 3/4". As much as I tried to stretch myself to be the tallest I could be, I didn't meet the height requirement. The woman who measured my height still passed me on, allowing me to dance for the audition and leaving me with a modicum of hope they wouldn't be strict with the requirement. When I left the audition, I remember trying to be Pollyanna and believe this tiny ¾ of an inch was not a problem. After all, it wasn't a full inch!

I remember the day I received my letter stating that I hadn't been hired because of my height. I wept for hours with disappointment. Not getting a call back didn't have anything to do with my weight, nor my talent or technical skill. I was simply not the right size for the job. And it was devastating.

Other than my eating disorder, my first passion was always dance. I was of course disappointed about the Rockettes, but determined to not let that stop me from pursuing a dance career. It was this same passion that I used to fight my eating disorder, a fight I eventually won. Although it took many years to resume a lifestyle with healthy eating habits and a balanced diet, I was able to attend college and graduate in three years with two degrees in psychology and social work. I was able to channel the energy from the eating disorder into dance, college and relationships. But the hardest part was finding my identity, separate from the eating disorder and from being a dancer. I knew how to pursue a goal, but I wasn't familiar with the concept of appreciating the process of being a university student. The diploma was just one goal that would enable me to move on to the next goal. Life had always been one goal after the other, with little appreciation for anything but the achievement. Yet these achievements were never enough, much like the numbers on the scale.

After college I was unsure of what was next, so I became a flight attendant for a major airline. I had always loved to travel and one of the first serious romantic relationships was with an airline pilot. I wanted to travel the world with him and flying seemed like it would be lots of fun. I thought it would be an easy job for a few quick years – I'd continued to dance and pursue my dreams. After all, flight attendants only worked three days per week. It was the late 1970s when the weight standards were still in effect. Lining up to stand on the scale like a herd of cattle was part of the job requirement for us "Coffee, Tea or Me" girls. Stan Herman designed my first uniform. It was a rust colored, three-piece suit accessorized by a scarf with the United Airlines logo all around the border. It was quite ugly, but I loved it and proudly wore the uniform. I barely tipped the scale at the three-digit mark; although at the time, I considered myself to be completely recovered from my eating disorder. Reflecting back now, I see that I was still very selective in when and what I ate, but the airline loved my thin body and I felt good about being the "right" size.

When I was furloughed from the airline at the age of twenty-four, I moved to New York City to continue my love affair with dance. I wanted to take classes and audition for shows. I lived in a four-story house for women in the arts. There were dancers, singers, musicians and many students from School of American Ballet and Julliard. At the time, they did not have residence hall so young women would stay at the Swiss Town House on a beautiful tree-lined street off Central Park West, across from ABC studios. I immediately made friends and cherished the time that I lived there.

I began teaching dance for Henry LeTang, the famous

Broadway choreographer, at his studio on 49th and Broadway. I had taken classes with Henry from the time I was ten years old, and was intimately familiar with the studio. It was always bustling with dancers who flitted about while Henry accompanied them on piano. My job was to teach students the series of dances, an opportunity I relished.

Performing the time step was simple for me, but I was cut as soon as I finished dancing. The audition was for a replacement, so they were looking for dancers to fit the costumes of the departing dancer. Once again, I was being cut for my size, not my talent. And once again, I was devastated, but this time, I felt more optimistic about my future and realized that I needed to grow thicker skin.

Being a dancer was my ticket to travel the world as a dancer and live in faraway places. My first break came when I was twenty-five years old and had the opportunity to perform a ten-minute excerpt from "Sophisticated Ladies" at the world-renowned Mikado Theatre in the Akasaka district of Tokyo. Living in Tokyo was the highlight of my professional dance career. The resplendent theatre had 2,500 seats and a beautiful waterfall. Before each evening performance, there would be an extravagant water and light show at 8:30 and 10:30 pm. There was a rehearsal studio on the sixth floor, so we spent most of our time before shows perfecting our duet and technique. I loved the country, the people and the healthy Japanese food. I was dancing every day, and with all the calories that dancing burned up, was able to be freer with my food. Even though I still scrutinized my body on a daily basis in the mirror, making sure that my stomach was flat or that my ribs showed, I was beginning to feel more comfortable in my own skin. I was learning to let go of my identity as "the skinniest girl" or "the girl with anorexia" and allowing my identity to reemerge as a dancer. The passion that I had taken from dance and turned into my eating disorder was at last returning. The drive for eternal thinness was diminishing because other things in my life were more important.

When I was a child, I was always adamant that I would never teach dance or own a dance studio, but as they say, never say never. After several shows in Japan, the next goal on my list was to open a dance studio. I was thirty-two years old and had just bought my first house in Los Angeles. I decided I could not be without dance in my life so I set out to open a studio in the small sleepy suburb of Calabasas. At the time, there were no dance studios in town. What began as a small, one-room space with zero students grew into a vibrant studio with hundreds of enthusiastic and dedicated students.

Never without a new goal on my wings, I decided to go back to graduate school for psychology. I wanted to be able to help others the way my therapist had helped me recover from my anorexia. While in school, I earned a master's degree in clinical psychology and along the way, took a class on eating disorders,. I had never studied eating disorders; I had only lived with one. Sitting in the classroom, I felt as though the professor was describing and dissecting parts of my life.

It was soon after this period that I started my work at Monte Nido Residential Treatment Center. I had attended psychotherapy for many years, but only after I had my own insurance through the airlines. Since there were no treatment centers for eating disorders when I was sick, I had never been around anyone else who had an eating disorder. Sitting in various groups, I listened to the girls and women who spoke about the prisons they lived in and the drill sergeants in their heads. I began to realize that I was so lucky I had escaped the confines of anorexia nervosa. One of the reasons that I love the Monte Nido philosophy is they believe you can be fully recovered. Many of the staff were recovered, including the owner and founder, Carolyn Costin. I began to understand how important it is for women to have role models who hold the light and the hope, when it's difficult or impossible to hold it for themselves.

I spent seven wonderful years at Monte Nido as an intern and a licensed therapist working with women who were suffering with bulimia, anorexia and exercise addiction. It was during this time that I realized I had a new kind of passion for the work I was doing, even though I was still running my studio and teaching dance. This newfound passion became more apparent to me as I guided people like a beacon of light through the dark tunnel of their eating disorder. It is so important for people suffering with eating disorders to learn to use their voice to communicate their needs. Many eating disorder patients use eating disorder behaviors such as restricting, purging, exercising or binging as a way to numb their feelings. A disconnect develops between the mind and the body. When someone is able to tune into their feelings and then communicate them verbally instead of through unhealthy behaviors, it's the beginning of the healing process. Of course, there are many other techniques and coping skills that I'll talk about throughout the book.

During all this work as a psychotherapist, flight attendant, dance teacher and business owner, I was beginning to recognize the need for more time for myself. This concept was very unfamiliar to me until I began my work at Monte Nido. I'd always been taught that not putting others first was selfish. But now I was learning to implement a model of self care into my life, similar to the one I'd explained many times in airplane safety demonstrations: "Put your own oxygen mask on first before your child's."

I spent five years as the Clinical Director of the Eating Disorder Center of California (a partial hospitalization program and intensive outpatient program associated with Monte Nido & Affiliates). Currently, I am the Director of Day Treatment Services for Monte Nido and have the opportunity to travel around the country making sure that all the day treatments are following the center's philosophy.

From a young age, a dancer learns to push her abilities to the limits. Teachers and choreographers are constantly asking dancers to lift their leg higher, turn more, leap higher, move faster, work harder. But there is always another dancer who can kick higher or who has better extensions. Thus each dancer is left feeling as though she's not good enough.

Perhaps you look in the mirror in a dance class to compare yourself to the other students, and your body looks larger—how do you respond? Your move is not as good as the person's next to you, or at least that's your perception, and you long to be better. What can you do? You audition for a job and really feel good about the way you danced, but you were cut. You scrutinize the audition in your head from the moment you walked through the door until the end of the audition. The recap leaves you questioning your own abilities as a dancer and you ask, *What did I do wrong?*

The identity of a dancer creates a distinct sense of self; much like the eating disorder becomes an identity. But what happens as the dancer ages? *Should I fear being fat if I'm not dancing the same amount of time I once did? Who am I without the eating disorder? What is my identity, if not a dancer?*

In these pages, you'll find many interviews with pre-professional and professional dancers. It's my hope that their cumulative knowledge and insider's insight help shed light on how to understand, prevent, treat and recover from eating disorders. These dancers, who come from different dance worlds and career stages, explore how dance has impacted their self-esteem and body image. Some of them had eating disorders. Others have struggled with body image because of comments made by a teacher or a choreographer that has stayed with the dancer for years. All of them have faced monumental pressures and, like myself in the past, have wondered, *When will I be good enough?*

# DÉVELOPPÉ...THE DEVELOPMENT OF AN EATING DISORDER

"My best friend in dance class began eating all salads and was not allowing herself to eat what the rest of the dancers would eat. I was worried about her, but I wasn't sure if that was eating healthy or she was developing an eating disorder."

—Carla, 13

N THE United States, 20 million women and 10 million men suffer from an eating disorder during some time in their life, including anorexia nervosa, bulimia nervosa, binge eating disorder, or an Eating Disorder Not Otherwise Specified (EDNOS) (Wade, Keski-Rahkonen, & Hudson, 2011). You may have heard of the different types of eating disorders and had some type of experience yourself, or perhaps know someone with an eating disorder.

If someone shows signs of an eating disorder, it's important they have a strong support system and find the right type of treatment. In this chapter, you'll find descriptions of the different types of eating disorders and how they affect the body.

This book is written for the dancer who has, or suspects they have, an eating disorder. Parents will also find the book informative. There's a chapter specifically written for guardians who need help dealing with how to approach the dancer when concerns arise about their health.

# WHY AN EATING DISORDER DEVELOPS

There are many reasons why someone develops an eating disorder. It can be thought of as "the perfect storm," when more than one of the following collectively happens in a person's life:

## 1. Genetic Predisposition – There is a genetic linkage on chromosome 1 (the largest human chromosome) for anorexia nervosa, according to Dorothy Grice, MD, of the University of Pennsylvania's Department of Psychiatry and Center for Neurobiology and Behavior. Current research suggests if a dancer's family member suffers from anorexia, their risk of suffering from the same eating disorder may be increased.

## 2. A Traumatic Life Event – This can be physical, emotional or sexual trauma. It can be an event that was difficult for someone, such as a divorce, moving to a new area, being bullied or experiencing a romantic break up. It may also include being teased for being overweight, or stem from the experience of being sent to a "fat" camp to lose weight. Remember that what is traumatic for one person may not be traumatic for another. It's all about the person's perspective.

## 3. Striving for Perfectionism – Many times, this is the temperament of a person with an eating disorder. They're striving for perfection in all areas of their life. They set the expectations for themselves and others extremely high.

## 4. Media and Societal Pressures to Look a Certain Way – Television, movies and magazine covers are filled with thin people, ways to diet and stay fit. The person who doesn't have an eating disorder can see ads, articles and films and not be affected. Someone with a predisposition to an eating disorder will compare themselves to others and believe that they do not measure up.

## 5. Family Communication Patterns – Families can have different communication patterns. Some families don't talk about feelings and emotions. In such a family, it's easy to begin to feel bad if there isn't an emotional response to something and if there's a discreet message that it isn't appropriate to share feelings. When feelings aren't addressed, a family member may feel the need to push their feelings down. Another family may fight and show emotion within the family, but then must present a good image to the world outside the four walls of their home. Portraying this "happy" family image can put a lot of pressure on someone.

## 6. Being Involved in a Sport Which Emphasizes the Body – Dance, gymnastics, wrestling, cheerleading, swimming, rowing, figure skating, and cross-country running are all examples of sports that emphasize the size of an athlete's body. If a coach or teacher says something negative to a team member or student—for example, a dance teacher may tell a student they need to lose weight to look better in a costume or leotard—it can have a definite impact on the person.

## 7. Mood Disorders – Anxiety and depression

are very much a part of eating disorders. Anxiety is often associated with anorexia nervosa. There is a correlation between separation anxiety as a child and the development of anorexia nervosa. Food can be a way that an individual learns to deal with their depression. If someone feels bad, they turn to food for comfort. There is a direct connection between the emotional being and the behaviors used to make a person feel better.

## 8. Diet Gone Bad – Many times, the last part of

the puzzle is a diet that someone goes on to lose a few pounds becomes an unhealthy eating plan. They are unable to stop the diet, or they diet and then begin binging.

## TYPES OF EATING DISORDERS

## Anorexia Nervosa

Anorexia Nervosa comes from Latin words meaning "nervous inability to eat." Someone with anorexia nervosa has a complete fear of gaining weight. They restrict the food they eat and have a very low body weight. If they do eat food, they have compensatory behaviors to get rid of the food such as restriction, exercise or purging. Many times, someone with anorexia has a very distorted body image and can't look into the mirror accurately. Even though the person may be at a very low body weight, they see themselves as fat. This can be difficult to comprehend if you've never had an eating disorder. Families and loved ones need to understand that it's basically like looking through a different pair of glasses.

An individual with anorexia spends the majority of their time thinking about food and weight. While they're busy restricting their food intake, they love to feed others. They may spend hours looking for recipes or watching the Food Network on TV. They normally won't allow themselves to eat the food they make, but if they do, then they must get rid of it.

Anorexia is a very serious disorder, which can have numerous medical complications and can ultimately end in death. According to the Eating Disorder Coalition, anorexia nervosa has the largest mortality rate of any psychiatric disorder. Females with anorexia nervosa eventually lose the ability to have their menstrual cycle. They develop osteopenia due to the bone loss and eventually osteoporosis. There can be damage to the heart, kidneys and other organs. There may be low heart rate and low blood pressure. Someone at a low body weight may grow hair on their body (it develops to help keep the body warm) called lanugo. If there's been laxative abuse, there can be irregular bowel movements and constipation. The relentless pursuit of thinness is many times more important than the serious health complications that a person endures, thus the high mortality rate from anorexia nervosa.

The DSM-V (also known as the Diagnostic and Statistical Manual of Mental Disorders, Volume 5), which is what a therapist would use to see if someone meets the criteria for anorexia nervosa, states the following as criteria for diagnosis:

1. Restriction of energy intake relative to requirements, leading to significantly low body weight in context of age, sex, developmental trajectory, and physical health. Significantly low weight is defined as a weight that is less than minimally normal or, for children and adolescents, less than minimally expected.

2. Intense fear of gaining weight or of becoming fat, or persistent behavior that interferes with weight gain, even though at a significantly low weight.

3. Disturbance in the way in which one's body weight or shape is experienced, undue influence of body weight or shape on self evaluation, or persistent lack of recognition of the seriousness of the current low body weight.

Additionally, there are two different types of anorexia nervosa:

1. Restricting Type – Weight loss is accomplished primarily through dieting, fasting, and/or excessive exercise.

2. Binge-eating / Purge Type – Engages in recurrent episodes of binge eating or purging behavior such as self-induced vomiting or the misuse of laxatives, diuretics, or enemas.

Someone who is suffering from anorexia nervosa may be exercising excessively in addition to dancing. They are overly concerned about body size, weight, calorie and fat intake per day. Their personality may be someone who strives for perfection in all areas of their life, including their body. What may start off as an innocent diet can turn into a deadly disorder.

As a dancer, there's a lot of pressure and competition to be the best. Since the body is the instrument used to manifest the art form, keeping it in the best shape possible is very important.

"If I can just lose a little more weight then the teacher will pay more attention to me. It is clear that she puts the thinnest dancers in the front because they look the best in their tutu."

Those were the thoughts of Janie, a twelve-year-old striving to be a ballerina, as she stood in her dance class. It's these types of thoughts that can propel someone into a diet that may lead to an eating disorder. In Janie's case, it led her to many years of bulimia as well as self-doubt as a dancer. She went on to have a successful career as a Broadway dancer, but always worried about the size of her body.

# Bulimia Nervosa

Bulimia nervosa is when a person eats large quantities of food (binges) and rids of the food and calories by compensatory behaviors such as severe restricting, purging through vomiting, exercise, laxatives or using diuretics. Someone with bulimia nervosa also has excessive concern about their body and weight, oftentimes accompanied by depression. The behaviors are a way to reduce the anxiety and stress through the binging and purging. Some people with bulimia describe feeling empty. The food is a way in which they can fill up the emptiness, while the purging is a feeling of relief or a stress reduction.

Bulimia nervosa can be thought of as a "silent" disorder because there is so much shame associated with it. When someone has anorexia nervosa, it is very visible by the size of the body, but someone with bulimia will be of a normal body weight. The person will engage in behaviors behind closed doors so that others are not aware of what they are doing. Often loved ones have no idea that their child, sister or friend has an eating disorder.

Bulimia nervosa also has many medical complications and can result in death. Someone with bulimia nervosa will have mineral loss through the purging which will cause the electrolytes in the body to be off and can result in a heart attack or heart failure. The acid from the vomit can cause damage to the lining of the esophagus, causing tears or ruptures. The salivary glands become swollen and there can be tooth decay from the stomach acid in vomit. A female with bulimia nervosa may have irregular menstrual cycles. If there is laxative abuse, there can be irregular bowel movements and constipation.

The DSM V states the following as criteria for bulimia nervosa:

1. Recurrent episodes of binge eating. An episode of binge eating is characterized by both of the following:
a. Eating in a discrete period of time an amount of food that is definitely larger than what most individuals would eat in a similar period of time under similar circumstances.
b. A sense of lack of control over eating during the episode (i.e., a feeling that one cannot stop eating or control what or how much one is eating).
2. Recurrent inappropriate compensatory behaviors in order to prevent weight gain, such as self-induced vomiting; misuse of laxatives, diuretics, or other medications; fasting or excessive exercise.
3. The binge eating and inappropriate compensatory behaviors both occur, on average, at least once per week for 3 months.
4. Self-evaluation is unduly influenced by body shape and weight.
5. The disturbance does not occur exclusively during episodes of anorexia nervosa.

# Binge Eating Disorder

People who eat large quantities of food without following it with compensatory behaviors to rid the caloric intake are called binge eaters. Binge eating disorder has also been referred to as compulsive overeating, emotional eating or food addiction. Many binge eaters are overweight or obese. Obesity is not a direct result of binge eating. Obesity is a medical condition and can have many different causes.

Much like the other disorders, binge eating disorder has medical complications. There can be high blood pressure, high cholesterol and heart disease due to high triglyceride levels. In addition, a person with BED can develop Type 2 diabetes mellitus.

The DSM V states the following as criteria for Binge Eating Disorder:

1. Recurrent episodes of binge eating. An episode of binge eating is characterized by both of the following:
a. Eating in a discrete period of time an amount of food that is definitely larger than what most individuals would eat in a similar period of time under similar circumstances.
b. A sense of lack of control over eating during the episode (i.e., a feeling that one cannot stop eating or control what or how much one is eating).

2. The binge-eating episodes are associated with three or more of the following:
   a. Eating much more rapidly than normal.
   b. Eating until feeling uncomfortably full.
   c. Eating large amounts of food when not feeling physically hungry.
   d. Eating alone because of feeling embarrassed by how much one is eating.
   e. Feeling disgusted with oneself, depressed, or very guilty.

3. Marked distress regarding binge eating is present.

4. The binge eating occurs on average, at least once a week for 3 months.

5. The binge eating is not associated with the recurrent use of inappropriate compensatory behavior as in bulimia nervosa and does not occur exclusively during the course of bulimia nervosa and anorexia nervosa.

Someone can start with a different eating disorder and end up with a binge eating disorder due to deprivation of food. Natasha, a 15-year-old ballet student, lost weight because she was told she would look much better in her tutu because her hips were too big. She lost more than 25 pounds and was given lots of praise for her weight loss. Unfortunately, the deprivation from restricting her food intake, led her to begin binging. She gained back the 25 pounds and more. It took a lot of treatment before Natasha was able to fight her eating disorder thoughts and begin to explore what she wanted for her life. She no longer dances and is currently in college.

## THE UNDERLYING REASONS FOR EATING DISORDERS

All eating disorders can be viewed as on a continuum from anorexia nervosa, bulimia nervosa and binge eating disorder. People develop one eating disorder but might slide up and down the continuum from one disorder to another.

Anna, a fourteen-year-old dancer in therapy, was overweight and teased as a child for the size of her body. She began watching her diet and exercising at the gym to lose weight. She couldn't stop losing weight and by the time she arrived in therapy, she had developed anorexia nervosa.. She was very careful with the types of food she ate, had stopped having her menstrual cycle and was obsessed with working out. She received a lot of praise for her thinner body and the discipline needed to work out every day, but she'd taken it to the extreme. She went from binge eating disorder to anorexia.

All eating disorders are psychological disorders accompanied by underlying reasons why the person developed the eating disorder. If the underlying reasons are not addressed the person will continue to use the eating disorder behaviors as a way to cope with their emotions.

Denise, a fifteen-year-old dancer, was admitted to a treatment center for anorexia nervosa as an adolescent and sought therapy when she developed bulimia nervosa. She had restricted her food intake and lost a considerable amount of weight. She gained weight while in the treatment but when she left the treatment center, she began binging and purging. Denise was then diagnosed with bulimia nervosa because of her normal body weight. She hadn't dealt with what purpose her eating disorder served for her and slid on the continuum to another form of an eating disorder. This was a young woman who had a lot of shame about her bulimia, and idealized her anorexia.

How one begins to explore the underlying causes of an eating disorder and the purpose it serves in their life is the beginning of the recovery process. The eating disorder is a part of the person, but it is described as an unhealthy relationship with self. If you can think about how you may have a critical voice, the eating disorder's voice is very similar. Like a constant mental loop, this voice berates the person for what they did or did not do. An eating disorder may say things to a person such as:

*Why did you eat that much?*

*Your stomach is too big!*

*You're never going to fit into your costume.*

*You better go exercise to get rid of what you just ate.*

*You are the fattest person in the class.*

*The teacher is never going to put you in front because of the size of your thighs.*

*You can't wear your leotard today because you look disgusting.*

*If you just lost 5 more pounds you would look so much better!*

There are many ways to treat an eating disorder (discussed later in this book). One of the most effective tools is for the person to learn to fight the eating disorder thoughts. When a person begins to counteract the eating disorder thoughts, they have a hard time believing anything other than the eating disorder. The process of recovery is like a muscle you must begin to build. It takes time and working on it every day to develop the healthy part of the self that can counteract the overly dominant eating disorder thoughts.

Recovery is long process, but the length of time it takes to recover depends on the amount of time the person has lived with their eating disorder and the age at onset.

There is a commonality shared by eating disorders in the drive for perfection. Dancers are always pushing themselves to be the best that they can be and, many times, there's the belief that you're never good enough. This is a similar thought to the eating disorder, which is a critical part of self, striving for perfectionism. What is the price of perfectionism for the dancer? When the body is used as an instrument, there needs to be a connection between body and mind. Many times with an eating disorder, the connection is disconnected, which can definitely impact the performance of a dancer.

How does a dancer balance their life? The better balanced the life, the less likely the development of an eating disorder. But this is problematic because there is such a commitment to being a dancer. It can occupy so much time that it's hard to find time for friends and having fun.

An important part of this book is education for both dancers and those who have a relationship with a dancer. You'll find important information including a guide to healthy eating and nutrition for dancers, signs and symptoms of eating disorders for early detection, different types of treatment available, and the levels of treatment. You will also find information and insight into the dance world and what is expected of young dancers. The more information you have, the better it will equip you—or the dancer in your life—to be happy and healthy.

Being a dancer is such a gift! Whether you're standing at the barre in class or are performing in front of an audience, dance is a beautiful art form and being a dancer is a special path in life. An eating disorder can be a major detour off this path and detrimental to physical health. *TuTu Thin* provides insight and information needed to live a healthy life as a dancer.

# AND AGAIN, 5678...
# IT'S NEVER ENOUGH

"As I watched the attention given to other dancers in my class, I knew that I could never be thin enough."        —Jessica, 12

HEN YOU SUFFER from an eating disorder, you live with the mantra, *never enough*. Whether it's the number on the scale that could always be lower, or feeling as though you can never get enough food when binging, or believing you can never exercise enough, the concept remains a familiar thread in the life of someone who suffers from an eating disorder.

There is always someone better standing next to you in the mirror—someone with a better physique or a higher extension or more perfect feet. The critical mind works overtime, and can inhibit dancers from being able to perform their best at auditions and even in class. Not all dancers develop eating disorders, but they are twenty times more likely to than the general population. According to author Sharon McConville, ballet dancers have a significantly higher risk of developing eating disorders than their non-dancing peers[1], so much so that the prestigious Royal Ballet School in London, England, publishes a Nutrition Policy online[2] with a section that addresses the issue of identifying eating disorders in students at the school and the proper protocol to take if identified. This policy suggests that students are more likely to become eating disordered because of a tendency "to conform to the stereotype of the 'perfect dancer'" and explains that students are "compelled to spend several hours a day in front of large mirrors and are inclined to compare themselves to their peer group."[3]

Many dancers either struggle with an eating disorder or disordered eating to achieve the body desired by their teachers and choreographers. Instructors play an important role in bringing out the feelings that tell the story of dance. Dancers need constructive criticism to improve technique and strive to be the best they can, but someone who has the predisposition for an eating disorder can hear the critique as an affirmation in their head that they're just not enough. To help a dancer recover from an eating disorder, teachers, families and even the dancer must work together to understand and address the critical voice that says, *never enough*.

## The Demands of Dance Study on the Perfectionist

If you're a dance student, you continually push your limits further to be the best in the class. You want to be sure that the teacher, choreographer or director notice you. You constantly compare yourself to the other dancers because you understand that others, too, are comparing you to them. Questions and insecurities gang up to berate you: *The teacher recognized another dancer in class but not me. Am I taking enough classes? I can never take enough classes or improve my skill level enough, especially as a pre-professional.* Sometimes in the mind of the dancer with an eating disorder, what's said isn't what's heard.

For example, a teacher may give a dancer corrections to help them find their center. They instruct them to imagine the line that runs through their body and pull their tummy in and tighten their bottom. To a dancer who is self-conscious of their body, it could seem the teacher is telling them their tummy or bottom is too big. They might be looking in the mirror with a voice chirping in their head that says, "Look at your body compared to everyone else. You are so huge that the teacher was definitely talking about your stomach." Here are some other examples of eating disorder thoughts:

| WHAT'S SAID: | WHAT I HEAR: |
|---|---|
| "You need to take more classes before you can be on pointe." | **"You are too fat to be on pointe."** |
| "Straighten your leg and point your toe." | **"I'm no good"** |
| "Tighten your bottom." | **"I am flabby."** |
| "Three people in the front and four in the back." | **"You're not good enough to be in the front row."** |

Young dancers want to push the limit because they want to pursue their craft. Just as important as attending class is attending dance conventions and summer intensives, where students gain the critical ability to learn from different teachers. But these experiences can add pressure to the dancer who already feels that no matter how hard she works and how thin she stays, it is *never enough*.

If a student is strictly a ballet student with the hopes of pursuing a career as a ballet dancer, then attending summer ballet intensives is imperative. For many young ballet dancers, the summer intensive programs at ballet schools are an excellent educational opportunity where prestigious individuals in the ballet world may spot them. While these intensive programs are incredible places to mature as a dancer, the demands placed on a young dancer call for balance, as well as an understanding support network, to help the dancer thrive amid pressure.

It's quite possible you begin leaving your family at a young age to live in a foreign city for several weeks during the summer. The programs can take up to a year to audition for and the pressure can mount before you even leave. It's important to carefully choose a program that's a fit for your mental and physical well-being. Even after thoroughly reviewing a program and getting an acceptance letter, it's not unusual for a dancer to feel a new sense of stress as opposed to relief, because once you are accepted, you may question whether you could have gotten into a better program.

Most young ballet students dream of going to the School of American Ballet, the American Ballet Theatre, the San Francisco Ballet, the Houston Ballet, the Miami City Ballet or the Boston Ballet to study for the summer. Let's say you get in to another summer intensive. What now? Should you accept or wait to see if you get into one of the bigger companies' summer intensives? You think to yourself: *If I go to one of the better-known schools for the summer, will I be one of many and not really recognized like I might in a smaller program?* These are some of the questions a dancer faces as they decide which program to choose even after they've been selected. Selecting a summer intensive is very similar to being sure you get into the college that's right for you.

Once you're in a program, the worries about which level you'll be placed in start manifesting. Unfortunately, placement may not only be a measure of ability, but an indication of who has the "best" body type for the ballet world. Such was the experience of Ellen, who was a beautiful young dancer with long black hair and an angelic face. She loved ballet and dreamed of being with a ballet company some day.

When Ellen came home from a summer intensive for young dancers from ages nine to eleven, she told her mother she didn't believe she'd make it in the ballet world because she didn't have the right body type. When explored further, the young dancer explained that she and her friend had auditioned for their placement in the levels within the program. Ellen, who studied dance six days per week and was in advanced level classes at her school, was placed in the lowest of six levels: Level One. Her friend, who was a gymnast and took far fewer ballet classes than Ellen, was placed in Level Four.

With no explanation about the decision, Ellen began to compare herself to dancers in the higher levels. If she could do all the moves that they were able to do in the audition, then why wasn't she in a higher level? She knew that she was every bit as good as them, but she noticed that she didn't have the same body type as them. They had long legs and short torsos. They were very thin and appeared perfect in physique. "Talent is not enough," Ellen learned at an early age. "I need to have the perfect body!" This experience changed the course of Ellen's life. Her dream of becoming a ballet dancer was shattered. She continued to be accepted to other summer intensives for some of the best ballet companies and her belief about her body continued to solidify because she didn't make it to the higher levels. Ellen was a beautiful dancer in many areas of dance, but since her mind was set on being a ballet dancer, she eventually stopped dancing altogether.

## The Program Where You'll Excel:
## Choices for the Young Dancer

Getting into a reputable program is important, but as Ellen's story demonstrates, it's also important that the program is the right fit for the kind of dancer you are. For example, being accepted to The School of American Ballet is quite an accomplishment. You are obviously "spectacular" if they accept you, but if your body or feet aren't what they're looking for, then you may not get the attention you deserve. You benefit most from attending a reputable school that also fits both your style of dancing and your body type. Carefully research the schools you are interested in attending and focus on the ones where dancers like you do well. If you can, try to do the following:

- Be sure that you have researched all the schools, the curriculum, supervision and housing.

- If possible, visit the school and watch a class to give you the best understanding of what your summer will be like.

- Ask if anyone in your school or audition has ever attended the summer intensive.

- Find out what the meal plan is for dancers for the summer. Are students on their own?

- Learn about their policy around eating disorders. Are they educated about them?

- Check out *Dance Magazine*'s annual January issue dedicated to summer intensive auditions.

## Dance Conventions and Competitions: Fun Opportunities and More Pressure

Dance conventions also have summer workshops and intensives where students can audition. If a dance student is interested in all forms of dance—such as ballet, tap, jazz, hip hop, contemporary and lyrical— then attending dance conventions enables the young dancer to study with other teachers and choreographers while measuring their own abilities with students from across the country. Most dance conventions also have competitions where students can participate in different forms and styles of dance competitions within their age category. It's a great venue for students who want to push themselves and prepare for the life of a dancer, where every audition is a competition.

Unfortunately, dance competitions can also cause young students to feel bad if they don't do well. Just as auditions for professionals are very subjective, so are competitions for young dancers. When a dancer is young, a negative experience in competition can lead them to believe they aren't good enough and possibly end their desire to dance.

Transforming dance tradition is a heightened standard of athleticism. Not just about the art of dance anymore, competitions are now about how high you can jump or how many turns you can do in a row. These expectations promote the feeling of never enough because you can be an excellent dancer who dances from the heart and soul, but be unable to turn or jump enough in a routine to score as high as someone with more tricks than feeling in their dance.

Striving toward tough competition standards is a way of life for many young dancers. Your whole childhood can be dedicated to a competition team. When a young dancer is a member of dance team or company—whether it's at a dance studio, a high school, or a cheerleading team—they give up numerous opportunities to be a part of other school activities.

Sara, a young dancer treated for anorexia nervosa, was home schooled to allow her more time for dance classes. She was very thin with long legs and a distinct style as apparent as her eating disorder. She participated in many summer intensives as well as dance competitions for her dance studio. But her desire to dance came with a price. She lost contact with the friends she had in school before leaving to be home schooled. When Sara saw them, they had little in common to talk about. Her whole life was dancing, so it was difficult relating to their life as high school students. After all, her time was spent looking in the mirror and worrying about where she was going to study in the summer, while they were worried about exams, boyfriends, football games and popularity.

Sara was left with only friends from her dance classes, but she felt judged by them. They were competing for the same parts in dances and auditioning against each other for summer intensive placement, so were they really her friends? As her isolation grew, her eating disorder became her best friend.

She spent her life in front of the mirror with self-critical thoughts. Her teacher frequently told her that she needed to stay on a diet, so the eating disorder thoughts mounted as her weight dropped. With her new body garnering positive reinforcement, she continued to lose weight. But she was never able to find the place where she lost enough weight. Once her new friend the eating disorder became her best friend, she was unable to hear outside comments about losing too much weight. This is why having balance in a dancer's life is so important. The eating disorder is happy to take over a person's life to the point where it helps drown out the loneliness or feelings of insecurity.

## Is Bulimia the Answer to be the Best?

Lisa, a beautiful dancer with long brown hair, an angular face and a cute turned up nose, began competing in dance at a young age. She was eventually awarded a scholarship to a prestigious studio in Los Angeles. She always looked up to the older girls on the studio's competition team. When one of the older girls showed her how she kept her weight down by purging her food, the impressionable dancer began doing the same. Lisa was perfectionistic and wanted to be the best. Purging seemed like a winning situation because she could stay thin and eat whatever she wanted. Little did she know that this would continue for many years because whenever she stopped purging, her weight would escalate and she'd have to resume the deadly behaviors. She saw no way out of this vicious cycle. What seemed like the solution to a desire for perfection became a vortex of destruction with no road map to escape.

For anyone with an eating disorder, the cyclical behaviors become habitual and are monumentally hard to break without the help of a professional. For a dancer with an eating disorder, the vicious cycle above is amplified by the reality that their very employment may depend upon their size. This pressure isn't merely perceived; too often it's the harsh truth. *If I am not able to maintain the perfect size as a terrific dancer, then someone else will be there to take the spot.*

## More Spectacular

Professional dancers aren't exempt from the *never enough* mind-set. One Broadway dancer, Jessie, reports that she was always let down by what she saw in the mirror. She constantly desired to be more spectacular. Yet she already was spectacular. She had a very successful career dancing in several Broadway shows as well as dance companies that toured nationally, and still it wasn't enough. Spectacular was her goal, but she never felt she achieved it because of her body type. Jessie felt she had a good self-esteem, it's just that her body was never the one she wanted. As a young ballet student, she quickly recognized the ideal body type favored in class, and understood that she would never be thin enough to achieve the ideal. But she would do whatever it took to stay as thin as possible.

There was no definitive number, but as long as the number on the scale continued to decrease then she knew she'd be competitive with the other dancers in her class and at auditions. To accomplish this meant purging all her meals beginning when she was twelve years old. This went on for fifteen years, even after her first job dancing on Broadway.

# The Future: Dance without Disorder

A common theme emerges from these dancers, whether they had eating disorders, disordered eating, body image concerns, or the basic belief that it's *never enough*: they needed to control the size of their body in order to dance. Each dancer perceived a message that their ability as a dancer was not enough, and that they also must have a perfect body. Yet truth be told, it is possible to navigate through struggles with body image, eating disorders and the boundless desire to dance.

The dance world does not create the eating disorder, but it is part of the recipe that leads to an eating disorder. It is ironic perhaps that the same certain personality types prone to developing an eating disorder (such as the perfectionist) will also pursue a dancing career. For example, someone who is a perfectionist may really like that trait about themselves, because it's the same part that drives them to be as good as possible at everything they do. A hard worker does the work that's needed to accomplish a task and be satisfied with their work. A perfectionist will never be happy unless they're the best. The problem is that perfectionism does not exist. We are humans so we are not perfect! This is the cycle that keeps someone with an eating disorder stuck, while they strive for the impossible dream of perfectionism.

## Taking a Break

A father of a young male dancer, Bill, wanted to be sure that his son didn't burn out on his desire to dance at a young age. He'd allow his son to go away to summer intensives, conventions and competitions; but only if combined with family vacations to Europe. He believed his son needed time to rest his body and rejuvenate.

This is a wonderful concept. Dancers can work to stop embracing the fearful thought that if they don't take an extra class or go away to every summer intensive, they won't find success in the dance world. Taking a break once in a while can give your body a rest and allow the time to enjoy relationships in your life. Relationships with people other than dancers provide a way to escape (for even a day) from the pressures you feel to be successful; whether it's pressure at your studio, a dance competition or convention or an audition for the summer intensive.

Why do some dancers develop an eating disorder while others just struggle with their body image? Do we just accept that all dancers will always have some feelings of insecurity about their bodies, or do we accept that our society in general promotes a feeling of inadequacy? How can you have a healthy self-esteem and healthy body image?

Maybe you know someone in your studio that you admire? If so, try reaching out or making a connection. It's important to look up to dancers who have healthy lifestyles. Having healthy role models is crucial to all young dancers. What if the older dancer in the dance studio had been a role model for Lisa instead of teaching her how to throw up her food? Lisa probably wouldn't have felt bulimia was part of the healthy pathway to "be the best."

Balance is possible for dancers. The recipe is a combination of self-confidence, trust in self, support from loved ones, health, ability to communicate, and the nurturing of relationships.

[1] McConville, Sharon: Ballet Dancing and Eating Disorders. Eating Disorder Hope, Eating Disorder Information, Help and Resources, May 12, 2013

[2] The Royal Ballet School Nutrition Policy. http://www.royalballetschool.org.uk/wp-content/uploads/2013/10/Nutrition-Policy.pdf Accessed on January 14, 2015

[3] Thomas, JJ et al: Disordered eating attitudes and behaviours in ballet students: examination of environmental and individual risk factors. International Journal of Eating Disorders 2005;38:263-268

# WARNING SIGNS AND THE PREVENTION OF EATING DISORDERS FOR DANCERS

"I noticed that Holly spent more time in the bathroom and she was always taking showers."

—Patty, mother of a 14-year-old pre-professional dancer

THE SIGNS OF an eating disorder can be very discreet. It may be difficult to recognize an eating disorder in oneself or a loved one. It may also be easy to hide an eating disorder (at least at first) to friends and family members.

As a dancer concerned about your body, you might start a diet with the intention of losing a few pounds, but it can quickly become a downward spiral of deception. Obviously, not everyone who goes on a diet develops an eating disorder. As discussed in the Introduction, there are many reasons someone develops an eating disorder. No one chooses to have an eating disorder but there is a choice to recover.

Education about eating disorders is key for the dancer and their families. Early detection can be very helpful in the success of the treatment of any eating disorder.

## WHAT TO LOOK FOR

The signs and symptoms of an eating disorder are different for each disorder. It's important to keep in mind that symptoms may overlap from one disorder to another, and while someone may show signs of an eating disorder, it may never completely develop. For example, a teenage dancer might be cautious with food intake, but that's as far as it goes. Another wears oversized clothes because she's body conscious, but it never turns into an eating disorder. Awareness is so important in recognizing that a dancer could be in trouble with an eating disorder. Knowing what to look for is extremely helpful in early detection.

## Here are some signs and symptoms:

Weight loss seems like the obvious sign for an eating disorder, but is only visible in someone with anorexia nervosa, not bulimia or binge eating disorder. Many individuals wear oversized clothes so no one knows their secret. As a dancer, it can be a source of stress to hide weight loss, as most students wear tight-fitting clothing such as leotards, dance shorts and tights.

Someone captured by an eating disorder begins to obsess about food, weight, calories and their body size. The person typically weighs in on a scale multiple times per day. Cutting out certain foods due to fear of food and what's in it is very common. Carbohydrates are many times the first to go. As a dancer, this can be a problem as carbohydrates are what give a dancer the energy to dance and perform. Without certain food groups, their energy level and stamina are reduced.

The dancer may begin to isolate from the other dancers or his or her friends. An eating disorder can occupy a lot of time thinking about the food. The person might be eating very little food, but they'll be thinking about it. For example, there's always time for an anorexic to watch food shows on television, collect recipes, or cook and bake for others (but not eat the food they prepare).

Someone who isn't eating becomes irritable and cranky. They can become easily agitated by circumstances or by other people as they deprive themselves of nutrients and fuel for the body. They are operating on empty. They are hungry, but refuse to give in to the body's signals that it's time to eat.

The person with anorexia nervosa eats, but eats a very reduced amount of food. Portion sizes get cut down, meals skipped, calories and/or fat grams closely counted. Each person develops specific rules around their eating disorder, but these "3 Rs" are some common signs:

RULES
The rules a person develops are what dictate their existence in the world. These rules tell them how much to eat, how many calories, what times to eat, what food groups they are allowed to eat, and more. The rules develop over time so you may not notice the rules or rigidity right away.

RIGIDITY
Because of ongoing struggles to anything outside a certain comfort zone, rigidity is very common. It can range from eating something that is not part of the plan for the meal, the time the meal is eaten or any changed plans.

## RITUALS

Rituals are also very much a part of an eating disorder. There can be certain patterns a person follows when eating. For example, cutting up food into very small pieces. Perhaps it's eating one food group before the other. Hiding food or pushing food around the plate is common when forced to eat with the family. If someone is making them eat a food that isn't within their rules, it's very uncomfortable and the individual looks for ways to get rid of the food.

Leaving the table after meals on a regular basis is a definitive warning sign. The person must get rid of the caloric intake and need to do it within a certain time frame after they've eaten. Perhaps they run water in the sink so no one hears them purging their meal. When the eating disorder takes control, there is a desperation and fear that drive the need to get rid of the food.

Taking frequent showers is also a warning sign there is a problem. This unsuspecting method provides a way to vomit without anyone suspecting because the sound of shower water running blocks out the noise of the vomiting; unlike the obvious sound of a toilet flushing.

As mentioned in the Introduction, people can purge with both anorexia and bulimia. But while a person with anorexia nervosa may view dinner as a binge, someone with bulimia nervosa eats substantial quantities of food.

A person who is binging also goes through large quantities of food. Maybe they're spending lots of money at fast food restaurants and grocery stores, or eating lots of food out of the pantry. Food missing can be a sign that there is a problem. You may ask yourself, how can a dancer eat large amounts of food and still dance? It's possible by restricting throughout the day and binging at night. Binging can be followed by episodes of purging either by vomiting, exercise, laxatives or diuretics.

Exercise shouldn't be a problem since it's certainly something that is healthy. But someone who uses exercise as a means of purging their food exercises to the point of unhealthy excess. For a dancer, this can be a problem as they may be dancing all day and then running at night or going to the gym to get rid of the food they ate during day. Someone who has a problem with exercise addiction exercises in any climate. They also exercise if sick or injured to get rid of the food and so it doesn't sit in their stomach.

The cycle of restricting, binging and purging can be a vicious one that is difficult to break. A person restricts food intake in order to lose weight. Eventually, they're hungry and the deprivation leads to binging. They feel guilty about the food that's been eaten and must purge it. This is a difficult cycle to break once it begins.

Eating alone may become more common as the eating disorder progresses. If someone eats alone, they don't have to answer any questions about what they eat, the quantity, or deal with anything that gets in the way of a decision to vomit after the meal. The person may also begin to lie about whether they've already eaten so they're not forced to eat with someone.

Before the development of an eating disorder, someone might be the most honest person in the world.

Unfortunately, the eating disorder is manipulative and conniving so it pushes even the most honest individual to become a liar. The lies are a way to protect the eating disorder so that others will not have all the information. Developing an eating disorder is similar to belonging to a cult where someone has control over your thoughts. The eating disorder is the leader of the cult and is convincing the person to exhibit behaviors they probably never exhibited in the past.

When someone has an eating disorder, it's as if there are two parts to the person—the eating disorder self and the healthy self. It is this concept that's such an important part of the recovery process. The person with the eating disorder must increase the healthy part of their self-image to be able to combat the thoughts and beliefs imposed by the eating disorder.

In treatment, clients can work on eating-disorder self/healthy-self dialogues to help fight the thoughts. This is one of the most important coping skills a person can develop to help fight their eating disorder (see Chapter 5, *The Dancer and the Mirror... What is Behind the Perfectionism of the Dancer?*).

## How to Prevent the Development of an Eating Disorder

It is important to have a healthy idea of body image as a dancer. Some dancers may not believe this is possible in the dance world. Dancers are very critical of themselves and others, so recognizing how to develop confidence in self, and as a dancer, is key. Remember, your body is your instrument so you need to treat it with respect and admiration for what it allows you to do as a dancer.

Your dance teacher and dance studio should understand the benefits of healthy body image. Since you probably spend hours at the studio, the first person to notice any changes could be your dance teacher. Many times, dancers spend more time with their dance teacher and dance friends than they do with their family and school friends. It's important for those in the dance community to look out for one another and support a healthy lifestyle.

You can help create a healthy atmosphere by helping to educate others about the importance of a healthy self-image as a dancer. If you hear another dancer or teacher talking about diets, bad foods, or negatively about their body, try talking about how important our bodies are as dancers.

> "I knew I did not get a lead in the Nutcracker because my teacher did not like the way my thighs looked in the costume. She had me on the fat list on the office door of the studio."
>
> —Michelle, 15

Dance teachers should not criticize dancers for their bodies. Dancers come in all shapes and sizes and the focus should always be on what the dancer is doing, not what they look like. When a dance instructor comments on a student's weight loss, it gives the person attention for the weight loss and they feel noticed and special, which in turn can fuel the eating disorder.

Parents also need to be aware of anything at the studio that could be causing their young dancer to feel bad about themselves. Also, pay attention to a loss of desire to continue dancing. If there is any weight loss or change in feelings about dance, it's important to be aware of what is going on. Many times, parents don't stay around to watch the classes (especially if a dancer is there long hours) and are unaware of what's going on and how your dancer is feeling.

> "My 14-year-old daughter asked if she could go to Weight Watchers with me to help her look better in her leotard and in the mirror. It broke my heart as I realized the impact my feelings about my own body were having on my daughter. That was never my intention."
> —Betsy, concerned mother from Los Angeles

A mom, dad or guardian's negative self-talk about their body can have a negative impact on a child. If they are always on a diet or talking about " good and bad foods" it can definitely influence the young person in the household. Dancers need to see and learn acceptance and appreciation for the body. Children learn about food and nutrition from their families so setting a good example is important.

# CONNECTION AND COMMUNICATION

"I always look forward to talking to my mom after dance when she picks me up. It is our time to connect and talk about the events of the day."
—Nicole, 13-year-old dancer

Connection and communication is a key element in the recovery process and also in preventing an eating disorder. When a person develops an eating disorder, they develop an unhealthy connection with self-relationship. It's important that a person has connection with friends and family to prevent the development of the eating disorder.

It can be difficult for a dancer with a busy schedule to have meals with their family every night. Often, they're at the dance studio in the evening, during dinnertime. Having family meals is very important for connections within a family. If a family can find a time to come together, they have the ability to share what's going on with each person, and it helps build better communication and connection. A good goal is for families is to aim for one to three nights a week where they can come together—with everyone in the family knowing that being there is mandatory. In addition, a family can agree to have dinner a little later on dance nights so everyone can attend. As a family, talk to one another to decide what works best in your house, and allow both children and parents to come up with solutions.

Staying connected to friends who aren't involved in

dance can be a challenge to a dancer for several reasons. Finding time to spend with other friends means taking time from family, dance or homework. Also, sometimes it's difficult to relate to the non-dance friend. As a dancer, you may not have time to attend school dances, football games, etc. This can leave you feeling as though you don't fit in. Staying connected means looking for a common denominator that will help you stay friends outside the dance circle. For example, hanging out at the mall if you like to shop with a friend, or having a movie night because you enjoy the same genre of movies, can be something you share in common other than school activities.

## WHAT TO DO IF YOU SUSPECT SOMEONE HAS AN EATING DISORDER

If you believe you have an eating disorder, be honest with someone you are close to that you may need some professional help. The sooner you begin to explore the relationship with the eating disorder, the more your chances of recovery. It's a difficult decision to be open and honest about your eating disorder, but also one of the most important factors in the recovery process. You have to be honest with yourself, your family, friends and treatment professionals.

Allow them to understand your struggles and let them know how to help you. It's not unlike steering a tank through a minefield. Your eating disorder has many mines and explosives hidden throughout the minefield that will explode if you go too close. Each person has different triggers that can upset them. If the person with the eating disorder can explain to loved ones what is helpful to talk about and what isn't, then it helps them to avoid subjects that can be upsetting.

For example, if a parent continually talks about their body and the need to lose weight, it can be very upsetting to the person with an eating disorder. But unless he or she communicates that to the parent, they'll continue to repeat it and upset their child.

If you suspect another dancer or a loved one has an eating disorder, you want to approach them with love and curiosity. Perhaps the individual won't admit to the problem, but they know that you are noticing and concerned. This may cause them to want to be more open with you. If you notice a friend or family member lost weight, you could begin a dialogue with something like:

"I've noticed that you've been losing weight in the last few months. I hope everything is all right with you. I want you to know that I'm concerned and if there is anything I can do, please let me know."

It's important to frame comments in a positive way. Avoid putting the person on the defensive. This could make them go even more undercover with their behaviors. Here are some suggestions:

| INSTEAD OF SAYING: | TRY: |
| --- | --- |
| "You look so skinny!" | "I noticed you've lost some weight... Is everything okay with you?" |
| "Why don't you just eat?" | "I'm worried because you never seem to be hungry or want to eat with me." |
| "Why do you always go to the bathroom after you eat?" | "I noticed that you always go to the bathroom after you eat. I hope you're alright." |
| "Why aren't you spending time with your friends?" | "I noticed you're not seeing your friends... just checking, is everything okay? |

You can also address yourself and work on changing your inner thoughts from negative to positive.

| INSTEAD OF TELLING YOURSELF: | THINK: |
|---|---|
| "I hate my body and need to lose 10 pounds." | "My body allows me to dance and move my body in a very special way, so I need to appreciate it for what it does." |
| "I don't eat gluten or carbohydrates because I need to lose weight." | "Carbohydrates are important for energy and I should eat an appropriate amount every day." |
| "I ate too much today so I'm not going to eat tomorrow." | "I may have eaten too much today, but I need to eat regular meals tomorrow and not restrict. My body knows how to adjust to the extra food. I have to trust my body. I have the opportunity to make healthy eating choices every day." |

## Pursuit of Passion

As a dancer, there may be fear around others suspecting an eating disorder because it could have an impact on their ability to dance. If someone is losing weight, they could fear having their eating disorder discovered and not be allowed to dance. The dancer has to have the drive and desire to dance, the passion! This is very important if someone has an eating disorder; the passion that they once had needs to be rekindled to eliminate the eating disorder.

Jamie, a 19-year-old woman who spent time in a residential treatment center for eating disorders, forgot how much dance meant to her until she participated in a dance class at her treatment center. It reignited a passion she forgot she had since an eating disorder took control of her life. Jamie went on to recover from the disorder and continues to dance and teach dance. She views herself as a role model for young dancers.

Even if dancers have passion for what they do, an eating disorder can quickly steal it away from them, much like it did with Jamie. Someone engaged in eating disorder behaviors may not be strong enough to be dancing. It's important for them to remember what dancing once meant to them. The personality type of someone with an eating disorder can be very driven and convert what once was passion for dance, into an unrelenting passion to have the perfect body. This person is on a destructive path and needs the help of possible treatment professionals as well as friends and family to help with the recovery process.

You can find recommended organizations listed in Chapter 10 (Resources for Dancers) that provide treatment and valuable additional information to help you through the process of overcoming an eating disorder.

# THE DANCER AND THE MIRROR...

# ...WHAT IS BEHIND THE PERFECTIONISM OF THE DANCER?

"I knew when I saw the beautiful ballerina leap across the stage at Lincoln Center that I wanted to be a dancer...

...everything about her was perfect, and I knew I needed to be perfect in my body and my dancing so I could look like the ballerina on stage."

—Roxi, 12-year-old pre-professional ballet student from New Jersey

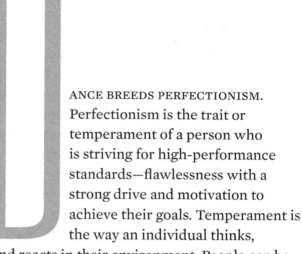

ANCE BREEDS PERFECTIONISM. Perfectionism is the trait or temperament of a person who is striving for high-performance standards—flawlessness with a strong drive and motivation to achieve their goals. Temperament is the way an individual thinks, behaves and reacts in their environment. People can be influenced by their environment as well as genetics. The perfectionist will have self-discipline, and an obsession with the end result. They are conscientious and have a great work ethic.

Perfectionism can be the trait that drives you to attend class every day; or get up early to get your homework finished so you can go to dance class after school; or drives you to spend extra time in the dance studio perfecting your turns and technique. The perfectionist is excellent with organization and time management to ensure his or her goals are obtained. A dancer may be in class 3-5 hours after school every night, but find time to complete all their homework for school the next day. They also find the time and make the commitment to getting all A's in school if it means being able to attend dance class every night. The professional dancer may no longer be in school but will continue this lifestyle of perfection. For example, a professional dancer may squeeze extra classes into an already jammed dance schedule to be sure they're ready for an upcoming audition. After all, in order to get the job they have to be the best. But once they get the job, they feel they can't let up—perhaps spending almost all their waking hours in the rehearsal studio perfecting choreography. And the pressure to maintain, or even improve their physique continues as they know an audience awaits them.

## Chasing the Rainbow

When a dancer stands at the barre with all the other dancers, each of them is striving for perfection. Perfection is what is perceived on stage, but there is a journey to get there. It's important for the dancer to master their technique, and working in class each day is a part of the journey. Setting realistic goals is important so a dancer doesn't apply so much "self-pressure" due to dance. The goal of focusing on the process as opposed to the end goal is very important for a dancer to understand. It is not an easy concept to grasp.

The goal to be the best dancer in the class or in the company is an example of how chasing perfectionism is like chasing a rainbow. The high standards that are set as a dancer will motivate the person to continue to push themselves beyond their capabilities to achieve the highest arabesque, the most turns, or the lead in a ballet or show. There is always a carrot that is dangling ahead of the dancer, even after achieving success. Sometimes this drive to achieve perfection can become detrimental to their work as a dancer, and eventually lead to an eating disorder.

The temperament of perfectionism is elevated in individuals with anorexia nervosa. The desire for control can be the beginning of the development of an eating disorder. For dancers, there are many things that are not in their control—such as their turnout from the hips, their flexibility, their feet, if they have the right arch in their foot, the length of their legs—that possibly contribute to success as a dancer. While these are all genetic components that could work against them, the dancer has to find others ways to work around their specific deficits and control those areas that are possible.

Body size is one area dancers can control. Perhaps a dancer starts off losing a little weight to look a certain way and get positive attention, but the drive for perfectionism pushes them forward to an unhealthy point. This drive is one of the many components of a "Perfect Storm" that can lead to the development of an eating disorder.

The expectation of teachers, choreographers and dancers themselves is for the dancer to be strong with a low body weight and have the ability to deliver perfection in their performance. If the dancer is able to recognize they do their best through hard work and acknowledge their achievements, then they have the ability to be adaptive in their drive for perfectionism. They can recognize and work toward obtainable goals. When a dancer takes perfecting their physique and technique to the extreme, there is a high risk for developing an eating disorder. According to Dr. Linda Hamilton in an interview with The New York Times, in the white middle-class population, on the average, 1 in 100 will develop an eating disorder. In the ballet world, 1 in 5 dancers will develop an eating disorder.

## The Price of Perfection

There is a dangerous line where perfectionism becomes problematic and the dancer begins to lose perspective. The dark side of perfectionism begins when a dancer believes that they are never good enough. No matter what they do, they never measure up. The standard the person holds is set so high, it becomes a problem. The standard is to be the perfect dancer, but this is unobtainable.

The dancer who has crossed the line believes that they can never make mistakes. They begin to fear they are letting others down when they do make mistakes. The feelings that ensue are those of shame and guilt, because they're not living up to the expectation of others, such as teacher or parents, or even peers.

They become hyper critical of themselves and always feel that they could be doing better. The thoughts become very black and white. For example, since they aren't perfect, they are a failure.

Some of the thoughts of a dancer who has taken their perfectionism to the extreme would be:

"I fell out of my turn going across the floor and I looked ridiculous."

"I know that I am the worst one in the class because it takes me a lot longer to pick up the choreography."

"I hate the way I did the combination across the floor. Everyone was staring at me, and I was horrible."

"I need to push myself harder or I will never be perfect."

"My turnout is worse than anyone in the class. That is why the teacher never looks at me at the barre."

"I completely blew the choreography and now the choreographer is never going to want to use me again."

The person who has thoughts like these begins to obsess about their abilities as a dancer and they constantly compare themselves to others in class. There is the fear of looking weak or silly in front of others. They must continue to challenge themselves. If they make a mistake, there is a fear of being chastised. The thoughts and drive for perfectionism is taken to the extreme, and the dancer begins to spin out of control. Dancing may no longer be enjoyable. The love that the person once had for dance starts to fade away. The occupation with weight begins to be what the dancer can control since they feel out of control in their dancing, or of what others think of them. The eating disorder is a distraction and a way to escape the fear that they won't succeed as a dancer. Ultimately, if the person is sick with an eating disorder they cannot dance and won't be able to compare themselves to others.

## Ali's Story

Ali, a twenty-year-old college student at a prominent Midwestern college known for its dance program, was thrilled when she was accepted there. She had danced since she was a young child and had always wanted to be a professional dancer. This was what she worked for her entire life. In high school, she didn't participate in activities at school because she spent every extra moment at the dance studio where she'd started dancing when she was three years old.

Ali had always been a thin girl, and even once she went through puberty, she had all the faculties for dance. She had beautiful long legs with great turnout and beautiful feet. Ali studied all forms of dance—tap, ballet, jazz, pointe, contemporary and acrobatics. She wanted to go on to dance on Broadway. She also studied voice to help her with her dream.

In the small dance studio south of San Francisco, she was always the best in her class. She danced with the same dancers from a young age. They were part of a competition team so they worked together as a group to deliver the best performance possible. The dancers always depended on Ali. And as the tallest and strongest dancer, she was the center.

Most of the girls on Ali's team went to college, but none of them really wanted to pursue dance. They enjoyed dancing but they had other ambitions. Yet the team admired Ali for her drive and determination. When she was accepted at the college of her choice, they were all very excited for her. They knew how hard she had worked.

Ali's dance teacher was like her second mom. She easily spent more time with her, and at the dance studio, than she did at home with her own family. Her dance teacher was instrumental in helping Ali find the perfect college for her to be able to pursue her dreams.

Ali's family was also very supportive of her dance. Her mother always wanted to be a dancer, but became pregnant with Ali when she was in college, and wasn't able to pursue her dance dream. She was not a stage mom, but definitely lived vicariously though her daughter. Her dad wasn't really involved in her dance world, but he attended all her performances and was very proud of how hard Ali worked to accomplish her goals. Ali's younger sister was also a dancer and hoped to follow in her sister's footsteps someday.

Ali loved college and was very happy in the dance department. The first year, they were mostly training and had one performance held at the end of the year. Ali was cast as one of the dancers in the ensemble. This was difficult for her because she was used to being front and center. In her entire life, she had been the best. Now, she was in an environment where she was one of many girls who were good dancers. She recognized it would require turning up the training to succeed as a professional dancer.

Ali auditioned for a summer program at a well-known New York City company. She had always wanted to live in New York, and was planning to move there after graduating from college. She had to convince her parents that this was what was best for her career in dance. They wanted her to come home to California for the summer, but Ali knew she needed to stay and turn up the notch on her training.

In New York, Ali attended classes all day at the intensive summer workshop program. Then she'd head over to classes at Steps on Broadway or the Broadway Dance Center. She was dancing over eight hours per day and having the time of her life. It was what she always dreamed about and wanted for herself.

She began to compare herself to the other dancers at the intensive workshop. She was good, but she needed to be better. She needed to push herself more and to be the best in the class. Ali was also recognizing how the other dancers were thinner than she was and they looked better in their dance clothes.

Ali never paid much attention to her body because she was always thin in comparison to everyone else she was dancing with. Even at college, she was thin compared to the others, but in New York City, the mecca of dance, she realized it would take losing a few pounds to measure up with the other dancers. She also felt that a few pounds would allow her to jump higher and have better lines in her movement.

Even with dancing eight-plus hours a day, she cut back on what she ate. She'd always had a good appetite and loved food. Her thought was to cut back about 500 calories per day. She began to pay more attention to what she was eating and how many calories were in her food. Ali thought if she lost five pounds, she would be happy and notice a difference in her body in the mirror.

Ali lost five pounds and then her belief was five more pounds would make her perfect. When Ali returned to school in the fall, everyone began to comment on her body and how amazing it looked.

It was the most attention she'd received since arriving at college and Ali loved it. She continued her weight-loss. Even though she lost the weight she originally planned on, she continued to believe perfection was just around the corner with each five pounds more that were lost.

Ali continued to push herself both in the dance studio and with weight loss. She was cast as one of the leads in the production for the end of the year. She was so excited, even inviting her family to come for the performance.

Ali was having problems with her foot every time she went on to relevé, but she ignored the pain and continued to push herself. After all, she strived for this her entire life. She was excited for the opening night of the four-night run of the show. Her family was flying in from the West Coast and she knew they would be so proud of her.

At the rehearsal on the day of the show, Ali was on stage and the teachers were praising her for how hard she worked on her technique and how great her physique looked. She was on top of the world.

During the performance on opening night, she landed

wrong on her foot at the end of the show. She was unable to walk, but she pushed herself to take the curtain call. She collapsed on the stage in tears. She could not move her ankle. She told herself she just needed to ice it and she would be fine. But that wasn't the case.

When her parents came backstage, they were startled by the appearance of their beautiful daughter. She was skeletal in her appearance and they could see every rib as she bent over to hold her ankle. They carried her to the car to take her to the hospital.

Ali had a fractured ankle and was diagnosed with anorexia nervosa. Her world came crashing down. Her dream of becoming a dancer was shattered. The ankle would heal, but it would be a long road back to recover from her eating disorder.

## How to Avoid the Illusion of Perfection

For Ali, the constant drive for perfection ended up costing her career in dance. She was unable to see that pushing herself to perfection was an illusion, which could end up in injury.

The dancer's body must be trained and also great care taken to keep it maintained. Dancers must to learn to dance smart and nourish their bodies with the proper foods (see Chapter 6, The Balanced Barre: Balancing Nutrition without Obsessing Over Calories) needed in order to perform on stage and in life.

Dancing is a constant learning opportunity. You want to be the best dancer you can be without putting too much pressure on yourself. Perfection is about achieving a goal regardless of the consequences.

A dancer must learn how to step out of their comfort zone of technique to achieve humanness. This is what the audience is going to connect with when they watch a dancer on stage. Most dancers can execute the moves, but it is the expression of the emotions through the body that is so important.

In dance today, there is tremendous focus on competition. To be a professional dancer, you must be able to compete. You will be competing with different dancers at all auditions. It is important for dancers not to lose the artistry of dance because of the pressure to do tricks in competition. When dancers focus on tricks instead of emotional connection to deliver the message, then the dancer misses that essential and key piece of humanness.

Strive to be the best dancer you can be. Compete with yourself and don't constantly compare yourself to others. When a teacher gives you a correction, listen and make the correction. Say thank you to any teacher who cares enough to give a correction. It means that they care about you as a dancer. Some teachers can be harsh in delivery, but know that there is good intention behind the correction.

Dance for the enjoyment of what you do. Allow yourself the motivation to achieve realistic expectations. Allow yourself the pleasure of recognizing your accomplishments. Being a dancer is something very special. Do not let the allure of being perfect steal your love of dance from you.

# THE BALANCED BARRE: BALANCING NUTRITION WITHOUT OBSESSING OVER CALORIES

"I need to lose some weight before the audition next week or they will never look at me for the Summer Intensive. I will need to really diet for the next week." —Kelsi, age 14

A S A DANCER, you need proper nutrition to fuel your body to perform at its best. It is important to learn from a young age to eat balanced meals for the rest of your life, as opposed to going on a crash diet for a certain role or audition. As an athlete, your body is your instrument so you need to keep it functioning well. This can be difficult because dance studios are often filled with obsessive talk about weight and new diets. It's important to have a solid sense of what you need to eat as a dancer and not engage in unhealthy dieting behavior. Being educated about nutrition and what to eat in order to maintain your weight as a dancer helps eliminate the chances of developing an eating disorder.

Eating disorders can start off as a simple diet that seems harmless. Many dancers share dieting tips with each other and being on a diet seems quite normal. Several dancers can go on a diet together, lose a few pounds and then stop; but the dancer who can't stop the diet becomes obsessed with their food. What starts off as cutting out a few calories continues to escalate into an obsession with weight, food and calories, and eventually an eating disorder.

The temperament of a dancer is one of perfectionism and achievement. Losing weight can become one of those achievements to pursue. In the beginning as a dancer, you may get a good deal of attention for losing weight and looking great, but with an eating disorder, you won't be "allowed" to stop and maintain a healthy weight. This is because you can never go low enough with the eating disorder mind.

Peyton, a 17-year-old dancer preparing for a professional career, was praised for her dancing but at one of her auditions was told she could lose a few pounds. Peyton began to be body-focused and began to lose weight. The choreographers suggested just a few pounds, but Peyton couldn't stop. She lost 25 pounds and an obsession with her body, food, and weight loss grew. What started off as a temporary diet turned into a dangerous eating disorder.

Whatever the eating disorder behaviors, the effects may not show up immediately, but overtime it can be devastating to your body. With poor nutritional habits, eating disorders can cause medical issues such as osteoporosis, or osteopenia, which is a bone disorder that leads to weakened bones and loss of bone mass. This can eventually lead to stress fractures that take the dancer out of class and performances. Other effects can be esophageal tears from purging food because the lining of the esophagus becomes thin. Eventually the esophagus can rupture and lead to death. Purging also causes electrolyte imbalances, changes in blood chemistry that cause fatigue, heart problems, and possibly death.

Low blood pressure and low heart rates are typical

for athletes. For someone with an eating disorder, the numbers can be even lower than the normal range for an athlete. Since this can be dangerous, the dancer may be asked to stop dancing altogether if readings fall below a normal range for their body.

Dancers with a low body weight can begin to lose the hair on their head and can also possibly begin to develop lanugo, a covering of fine hair on the rest of the body that grows to keep the body warm due to malnourishment. Other physical problems from eating disorders include the wearing away of enamel on teeth, with eventual tooth decay and possible loss of teeth from the acid that is caused from vomiting. Eating disorders can also cause intestinal and digestive issues. More information can be found about the effects of the eating disorder in Chapter 4 (*Warning Signs and the Prevention of Eating Disorders for Dancers*).

Learning to trust your body with food is an important part of learning to eat for the rest of your life. Dancers have to trust that their body knows what to do when they grand jeté across the floor and it's important they learn to listen to the hunger and fullness cues that are actually an inherent part of their bodies. A dancer who has developed an eating disorder has lost all connection with body cues that indicate when they're hungry and when they're full.

Leslie, a ballet dancer who has had anorexia since the age of 12, struggles with the ability to trust that her body knows what to do with food. Her fear is that if she follows the meal plan set for her by the dietician, she'll gain weight and her body will never stop gaining weight.

Leslie struggles to listen to her body's cues, but easily listens to the eating disorder voice in her head.

This voice can be hard to ignore and the dancer needs to begin to trust their body. Many times this can be accomplished with the help of a registered dietician and a therapist who specializes in the treatment of eating disorders. Please refer to Chapter 10 (Resources for Dancers) for suggestions about finding a treatment team, including a registered dietician.

A dancer who is recovering from an eating disorder may be restricted from dance until they reach a certain weight. At that time, they would be slowly returned to dance with certain restrictions until the weight restoration is complete and the dietician feels the dancer is comfortable with the meal plan. They may be placed on a maintenance meal plan to see if they can maintain the weight as they return to dance. Conversely, a dancer who has suffered from bulimia nervosa may not need to gain weight but must learn to follow a meal plan and not purge their food. The body needs to have time to stabilize fluids, electrolytes and metabolism.

As a dancer, you have additional nutritional needs due to the high level of exercise/energy spent in classes, rehearsals and performances. Dancers need a higher caloric intake than the average person. It is important as a dancer to focus on your own needs and not compare yourself to your friends, parents or family members who eat differently or not as much as you do. This can be difficult for a dancer with an eating disorder because they compare their food intake at a meal to others.

# Healthy Meal Plans for Dancers

A dancer can easily be burning 2000–4000 calories per day, depending on how long they are dancing, the intensity of the dance and their individualized energy needs. It is important to nourish your body throughout the day to keep the blood sugar levels consistent and protect muscle mass. A young dancer who is still growing needs potentially greater than 3000 calories per day to keep their body nourished and to continue to build bones. Educate yourself about what your body needs to be able to dance so many hours per day instead of obsessing about counting the calories you are ingesting. Too few calories will result in loss of muscle. Loss of muscle equals loss of strength. A nourished dancer is a strong dancer.

A dancer should recognize that food gives the body energy, not caffeine or supplements. For example, a latte may seem filling and give you a temporary shot of energy, but it doesn't supply the nutrition a dancer needs to fuel the body during 4-6 hours of rehearsals and performances.

It's very important that dancers consume bone-building nutrients daily, including:

Calcium
1200 – 1500 mg daily
Found in: milk, yogurt, cheese, kale, spinach, white beans, soybeans, green leafy vegetables and almonds.

Vitamin C
100 mg daily
Found in: orange juice, oranges, strawberries, papayas, broccoli and cauliflower.

Vitamin D
10 – 15 mcg (400 – 800 IU), or get 15 minutes of sun daily
Found in: tuna, salmon, cheese, fortified milk and egg yolks.

Vitamin K
75 – 90 mcg daily
Found in: broccoli, asparagus, green onions and Brussels sprouts.

Omega 3's
1.5 – 2 grams daily
Found in: walnuts, salmon, trout, herring and flaxseed.

Potassium 1
250 mg daily
Found in: bananas apricots, avocados, lima beans, soybeans and potatoes.

# The Importance of Protein

Protein is essential for muscle strength, the ability to fight infection, the production of hormone and enzymes, as well as aiding in the ability to repair injuries.Protein also helps the dancer feel satisfied between meals because it digests and metabolizes more slowly than carbohydrates. A female dancer needs between 60-80 grams of protein per day. Protein sources would include: beef, chicken, fish, dairy products, tofu, almonds and peanuts.

It is important to note that young dancers have special nutritional needs to help with their growth and development. They require extra calories in addition to those needed for daily exercise.

These ranges may change based on individualized needs. Check with a dietician for your exact range.

# Balanced Meal Plans

The most important part of balanced eating is to eat regular meals and snacks. All meals should consist of a macronutrient balance of proteins, fats and carbohydrates, as well as fruits and vegetables.

If you look at a plate of food and divide it into three sections, one quarter should be the protein; one quarter should be the carbohydrate grains; and half of the plate should be fruits and vegetables.

The fat should appear as appropriate in the preparation addition to the meal. Fat used in cooking, such as olive oil or added to a food item such as an avocado, adds flavor as well as nutrition such as fat-soluble vitamins and essential fatty acids.

## Breakfast Options:

1. $\frac{1}{2}$ cup of granola, 1 banana, 2 Tbsp of almonds, 1 cup of 2% milk or vanilla soymilk

2. 1 bagel with 2 Tbsp cream cheese, 1 cup of 2% milk or vanilla soymilk

3. 1 cup of Greek yogurt, 1/4 cup of granola, 1 cup of berries and 1-2 Tbsp of seeds (chia or flax)

4. 1 English muffin with 2 Tbsp of peanut butter, 1 cup of 2% milk or soymilk, 1 tsp of butter or margarine, 1 apple, orange, pear or banana

5. $^2/_3$ cup of oatmeal, 1 cup of 2% milk,
   6 almonds or cashews, $^1/_4$ cup of raisins

6. 1 egg sandwich: 2 slices of bread, 1 whole egg,
   1 oz of cheese, 1 cup of orange juice

7. 2 Eggo waffles with 2 Tbsp syrup, 1 cup of
   2% milk or soymilk, strawberries

## Lunch Options:

1. 2 slices of bread or 1 pita, 4 oz of tuna with
   2 Tbsp of low-fat mayo and 1 large cookie, small
   bag of chips or 1 cup of flavored low-fat yogurt

2. 1 cup of salad, $^1/_2$ cup of kidney beans,
   3 oz of turkey or 3 oz of soy meat slices, 1 Tbsp
   of regular salad dressing, 1 cookie or 1 serving
   of fruit

3. 2 cups of pasta salad with chicken or tofu and
   vegetables, 2 Tbsp of regular dressing, 1 serving
   of fruit

4. $^2/_3$ cup of tuna or egg salad with mayonnaise,
   lettuce, tomato, baby carrots, sweet pickle
   chips, ciabatta roll and a small bag of chips or a
   medium-sized cookie

5. 1 cup of fresh fruit salsa, 1 cup of low-fat yogurt
   or cottage cheese, 1 bagel with 1 tsp of butter or
   margarine or 1 Tbsp of peanut or almond butter

6. 4 oz of chicken or tofu, 2 tbsp toasted cashews, 1 cup of mixed greens with chives, 2 Tbsp of Chinese dressing, $1/4$ cup of crispy noodles

7. 4 oz turkey or soy meat, 1 oz mozzarella, Swiss, or provolone cheese, 1 pita, lettuce and tomato slices, 1 serving of fresh fruit or 6 oz of fruit juice, 2 tsp regular mayonnaise, 2 oz of avocado

## Dinner Options:

1. 6 oz of grilled shrimp or tofu, $2/3$ cup of rice, 1 cup of cooked vegetables in cooking oil, $1/2$ cup low-fat ice cream or 1 large cookie

2. 4 oz grilled chicken breast, 1 cup of salad greens, 1 whole-wheat roll, 1 tsp of butter, 1 Tbsp of regular dressing, 1 large cookie or $1/2$ cup of low-fat ice cream

## Always Be Prepared

As a dancer, it's so important to have food with you during the day. Plan out your day the night before and include all meals and snacks. Be sure that you leave enough time to eat your food and take snacks and meals with you. If you are rehearsing or in class, you might run late so always be prepared. Remember that food is fuel for your body to be able to dance and perform. Dancers who are prepared each day with meals and snacks are able to be flexible. Avoid going more than 2-3 hours without a meal or snack. You don't have to be perfect with your food, but consistency is very important. Remember to listen to your body—hunger and fullness are built in regulators, we just have to learn to listen.

3. 1 turkey burger or veggie burger, 1 whole-wheat bun, 1 slice of regular cheese or 2 slices of soy cheese, 1 cup of salad with 1 Tbsp of regular dressing, 1 serving of French fries or sweet potato fries

4. 6 oz of grilled fish or shrimp with olive oil, $2/3$ cup of brown rice, 1 cup of salad, 1 Tbsp of regular dressing, 1 serving of fruit

5. 1 yam or baked potato, $1/4$ cup of sour cream, $1/4$ cup of shredded cheese and 1 cup of broccoli with 1 Tbsp of regular dressing

6. 1 burrito tortilla, 4 oz of ground turkey, 1 cup of lettuce, tomato and onions, $1/4$ cup of shredded cheese, 2 Tbsp sour cream, 3 Tbsp salsa, 1 serving of fruit

7. 2 slices of medium pizza and 1 cup of salad with regular dressing

8. 1 square of lasagna with 1 cup of salad and regular dressing

## Satisfying Snack Options:

1. $1/3$ cup of trail mix

2. $1/3$ cup of hummus and 18 Wheat Thins

3. 1 Promax Bar – Cookies 'n Cream or Nutty Butter Crisp

4. 1 serving of fruit (1 apple or 1 orange or $^1/_2$ banana or $^1/_2$ cup of grapes and $1^1/_2$ cups of low-fat cottage cheese

5. 1 cup of yogurt and $^1/_4$ cup of granola

6. 12 Wheat Thins and 2 pieces of string cheese

7. 1 large cookie and 1 cup of 2% milk or vanilla soymilk

8. $^1/_3$ cup of nuts (almonds and cashews) and 1 cup of apple or orange juice

9. 1 Luna bar and 1 cup of 2% milk or vanilla soymilk

10. $1^1/_2$ cups of ice cream

# ON POINTE: FINDING THE BALANCE BETWEEN DANCE AND LIFE

"Dancing was my life until I was injured and realized I needed to have other interests to help balance my life."
—Holly, a 21-year-old dance student, hoping for a professional career

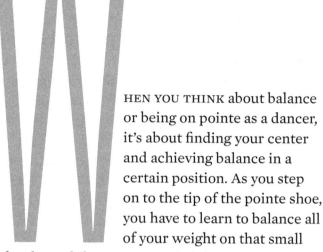

HEN YOU THINK about balance or being on pointe as a dancer, it's about finding your center and achieving balance in a certain position. As you step on to the tip of the pointe shoe, you have to learn to balance all of your weight on that small area of the shoe while you turn and glide across the studio. The definition of balance is the "distribution of weight enabling someone or something to remain upright and steady." This is what a dancer is doing all the time in the studio and on stage.

Dancers work on perfecting the ability to balance each day in dance class, but how do they learn to balance their life both inside the dance studio and outside? To be a dancer, there is an expectation that you will do whatever you need in order to perfect your body, technique and performance. But how does this allow time to enjoy other things in life such as time with friends, family, vacations and school? It can be challenging but there are ways to find a balance.

## WITHOUT A BALANCE

When a dancer does not have balance or perspective, they may begin to be obsessive. This obsession can manifest itself in the pursuit of being the perfect dancer, having the perfect body or pursuing the ideal role in the next show. It is the lack of balance in life—often including nutrition, sleep, and relationships—that can lead a dancer down a negative path.

If a dancer is only focused on becoming a dancer, and most of their time is spent in the studio, there isn't a lot of time for relationships. This is when an unhealthy relationship with oneself can possibly begin to develop, and it becomes an escape from the pressure and stress to succeed. Along with a teetering lack of balance, there's no outlet for emotions. The development of an eating disorder serves as a method to be able to numb out and mask the disappointment that can come with working hard and not getting the recognition.

Maybe your teacher isn't correcting you in class, or didn't cast you in an upcoming performance. Isn't he or she seeing how much extra time you are spending in the studio? Don't they realize how much you've prepared for auditions? This frustration can fuel the eating-disorder mind.

An eating disorder is a way to not have to worry about whether you are successful because you will be too sick to perform. It is certainly not the intention when one develops an eating disorder, but it's definitely one of the end results. It also guarantees an unbalanced life as the eating disorder takes over and doesn't allow you to have other relationships or do things that you enjoy.

## ASSESSING WHAT'S IMPORTANT

As a young dancer dreaming of dancing professionally one day, you face many choices. As you progress, you're required to take more classes, which takes time from other activities that you may want to participate in, leaving it up to you to make choices. Your dance teacher may require you take a certain number of classes in order to be a member of the company, but you may want to participate in a sport, which also has certain requirements. What do you do? Is it possible to balance both? The answers depend on your situation and your priorities.

No matter who you are, fun is an important part of the equation in the quest to find balance. Find other activities that you enjoy doing. It may be reading, watching movies, listening to music, watching your favorite TV show, or walking your dog on the beach. Whatever you enjoy, be sure that you find time for it in your busy life.

Finding time for other activities allows you to enjoy your time in the studio even more. It also gives you time to rest your body. Knowing how to give your body time to recuperate from a long day of classes or rehearsals is part of learning balance. Creating a schedule and allotting time for activities outside of dance can help you "commit" to fun. If you can't find a full Saturday afternoon that's free because of dance classes or rehearsals, work on shorter activities throughout the week. Even a one-hour activity a few times a week can create a big difference. Making a life outside of dance can help your mindset both in and out of the studio.

## Friends In and Out of the Studio

As a young dancer, it's important to have friends at the dance studio and also at school. Friends at the dance studio understand what you're going through in class, but they are also the dancers you'll be competing with for different parts in local shows. What's more, they may be the dancers comparing themselves to you in the mirror.

Friends from school may not understand the pressure you feel to be successful in the dance studio, but they'll hopefully support you in your endeavors by attending performances and also offer other opportunities outside the dance studio for socialization and fun. Some of your school friends most likely have their own passions—horseback riding, ice-skating, soccer—and you can connect by talking about their goals. They might even open up a new hobby or activity for you to enjoy.

\*\*\*

Below is the story of Kasey, who took time to enjoy her high school years before becoming serious about her dance career.

# Kasey

Kasey had been dancing since she was three years old and loved it. She was very involved in the dance team at her dance studio, but able to find time for friends, school activities, church choir and family. When she was ready to go to high school, Kasey wanted to be a cheerleader for her high school team. Her dance training had prepared her for the audition, which included a lot of acrobatics and aerial work. Kasey decided that she wanted to give her cheerleading squad all of her attention, so she left dance to be a cheerleader. Her dance teacher was so disappointed and Kasey was sad that she had to choose between the two activities. But she also knew she needed to focus on schoolwork and one activity was more than enough to keep her busy.

Kasey missed dance, yet felt she was able to spend time with friends and be involved in activities in her high school. She was homecoming queen and had a lot of friends. Kasey continued to be a cheerleader throughout high school and then eventually returned to dance in college. She majored in business, but attended many dance classes at school and at a nearby studio. She forgot how much she loved dance. After college, she moved to New York and began auditioning for shows. It wasn't long before she was cast in the chorus of a national tour. She loved what she was doing, but also realized that her break from dance had given her a much different perspective. Kasey truly believes she might not have moved to New York to be a dancer had she continued dance throughout high school.

Allowing herself to experience other things—such as cheerleading, boyfriends, school dances and homecoming—gave her a normal high school life. When you dance all the time, you may take it for granted. Kasey loved high school and learned how much dancing really meant to her. And she was lucky she didn't lose a lot of her technique and extension and was able to live the life of a dancer on a national tour.

She enjoyed visiting new cities and learning all about what it takes to prep the show in each city. She always looked for a place to take dance class as soon as she arrived in a new location. She loved experiencing new teachers and classes. She also spent a lot of time taking photos of different cities. Photography was a hobby she really enjoyed when she was away from the dance studio or on the stage. It was another way to experience looking at life outside of the studio. This was her balance.

## Recharging Your Battery

Learning how to take care of yourself is an important part of being a dancer. After all, your body needs to be cared for in order to perform. Being a dancer is an identity, a way of life.

Listening to your body and what it needs is not always as easy as one would think. As dancers, we are asked to push our bodies to the limit. But constantly pushing the boundaries can leave the dancer with a lack of awareness about what they actually need outside of the dance studio.

When you dance all day, you need to be sure that you know how to nourish your body. This doesn't mean just eating the right foods; it is about finding different ways to feed your mind, body and soul outside of the studio.

As a dancer you have to have a connection between the mind and body to be able to perform the choreography technically, but with heart. Knowing how to balance your life outside the dance studio is just as important.

Relaxation is key to being able to balance your life as a dancer. Maybe it's about having coffee with a friend or about cuddling up with a good book or movie on your day off. Find things that make you smile and that you enjoy. After a day of long rehearsals or classes, a hot bubble bath is a way to relax and soak sore muscles at the same time. Yoga is another way to connect the mind and body and at the same time give your body strength and conditioning that is different from a dance class. Using a journal to write your experiences is also something that can be extremely helpful whether you are still living at home or traveling around the world. It can be a great way to keep track and record all the memories of your life as a dancer. Allow it to be your companion instead of an eating disorder.

Be sure that you also have friends or family members who understand your life as a dancer. Being able to share moments of joy as well as your concerns and worries with someone is a way to release stress from your body.

\*\*\*

Here you will find the story of Ethan, who knew he wanted to be a dancer from a young age. He was persistent and driven, but also found ways to balance his life on his journey as a dancer.

## Ethan

Ethan began dancing at the age of five. It began when his mother recognized his abilities as she tried to teach the family a dance step she had learned in another country. He was the only one in the family who could pick up the step and so she started him in dance classes. He loved dancing and displayed a lot of talent. His dance teacher asked his mom to have him audition for the dance company. He began dancing 8-10 hours per week. When he went to middle school, he would walk to the studio after school, complete his homework and then dance until the studio closed. His parents had European ties so every other year the family would spend the summer in Europe. This gave him a break from dance and allowed him to rejuvenate for the upcoming season.

Ethan auditioned for the performing arts high school in Los Angeles. He was accepted. He rode the bus every morning to school, which included several transfers to complete the trip, about 30 miles from home. Ethan did this commute for four years. He also continued to perform with his studio dance company.

His hard work paid off and he was accepted at Julliard to continue his training in college. He continued to work hard through college with his eyes set on a professional career. Ethan enjoyed his summers where he would take time to relax at home with his family and friends. This was the period to recharge his battery, while allowing himself some downtime from dance. He was accepted into a company after graduation so his dedication helped him obtain his goal. Dancing was always a priority in Ethan's life, but he also made time for family, friends, vacations and self-care.

## Life on The Road

For the traveling dancer, much of your life can be spent out of a suitcase. How do you manage life on the road, and how do you cope with loneliness and strained relationships without disordered eating? When you are living in a hotel room in a strange city, how do you occupy your time when you're not performing or rehearsing?

Exploring a new city can be a great way to get to know your surroundings. Life on the road can be exciting and sometimes lonely. A dance class or yoga class can allow you to enjoy your time in a new city. Staying in touch with friends and family will help you feel more connected. Your journal can be your friend while helping you narrate your story.

*** 

Lexi spent a lot of time on the road at a young age. She lived away from her family at the age of fifteen because she wanted to be a dancer. She had to work on finding balance in a life that was driven by dance at a young age. Here is her story.

## Lexi

Lexi was a fifteen-year-old ballet student who wanted to pursue her career as a ballerina. She began dancing when she was eight years old. She moved through the levels quickly and began to excel. Her teacher felt that Lexi should participate in a summer program. Over the next few years she went to several summer programs.

Lexi moved to San Diego full-time to be able to study dance every day without any distractions. She completed her high school education through a correspondence course. She graduated from high school by the time her parents dropped her off in New York City to begin her study at The School of American Ballet.

Lexi had given up her high school experience to pursue her dream of becoming a ballerina in a famous company. Her dream came true, and by the age of sixteen she was on stage dancing as a member of the corps de ballet with a major ballet company in New York. She was living her dream, and although she had given up football games and boyfriends, she was living the life she'd imagined as a child.

Lexi put all her energy into dance and felt it paid off in her life as a dancer in New York. But it was time to learn how to find balance while touring the country and living out of a suitcase for several months out of the year. It was important for her to stay in touch with family while she was on the road. And it was important for her to write to her friends from New York and home so she felt connected to people other than those in the company she spent every day with in rehearsal and performance.

She also read a lot of books, which she enjoyed because it allowed her to rest her body while using her mind. She had never attended college, but wanted to continue to learn and educate herself about things other than dance.

Lexi loved to travel, so visiting different states and countries was very exciting. Since she was determined to get to know each city, she often wandered the streets to explore and understand the culture of each destination.

What Lexi loved the most was dance, but the added bonus was her chance to see the world on tour. When she returned to New York, she took vacations when on hiatus from performance. Even if she had planned her life, she couldn't have asked for anything better.

\*\*\*

Dance incorporates mind, body and spirit in the art form. Learning to find all of it within yourself, and how to balance your internal struggle along with external pressures to find balance for your life (separate from dance) can be a challenge. But this is the journey we are all on as dancers. It is never about the end result being the perfect job or gig, but about the journey we embark upon to find each job.

On that journey, we also need to develop the balance

within oneself to sustain the ability to tolerate rejection as well as accomplishments.

If you find that balance as a dancer, you will believe in yourself and know that you are proud of what you accomplish. It also allows you to have the belief in your talents, which lessens the stress, insecurities and pressure you feel to succeed. It becomes about the journey to be on pointe!

# TREATMENT OPTIONS FOR THE DANCER

"Making the decision to leave
the dance studio was one of
the hardest decisions I have
ever made, but it changed
my life in such a positive way
that I am happy that I had
the opportunity to attend
treatment."

—Trista, a 17-year-old
dancer who suffered from
anorexia nervosa

THE DECISION TO go into treatment is a difficult decision. If you are an adolescent, your parent or guardian will probably make the decision for you. As an adult, you always have the choice. If you are struggling with an eating disorder, then it is not only you making the decision. Instead it's the deceptive, manipulative part of yourself that we call the eating disorder that pushes you to not attend treatment for fear that you may actually begin the recovery process. It's the voice in your head telling you that you aren't sick enough to need any form of treatment. This voice is trying to deceive you so that you continue to listen to the eating disorder. The right treatment team can help you start to fight the thoughts and voices and explore the underlying causes for the eating disorder.

Once you begin the search for treatment options, be sure you understand and know the level of care that would be best for your eating disorder symptoms. If you do an intake at a treatment facility, they'll be able to give you a better idea of the level of care they would recommend. It is important to complete an intake, but this process is not a commitment to that particular treatment center. Be sure that you have done your research and feel comfortable with your selection. A recommendation for treatment may come from a family member or friend. Maybe they know someone who went to a certain treatment center. If you are in outpatient therapy, your therapist and dietician may have some recommendations for you. There are different levels of treatment depending on the severity of the eating disorder. Below you can find the different levels of care (from the lowest intensity to the most acute), a brief description of what the level of care entails and the criteria used for each level of treatment.

1. Outpatient Therapy
    a. Treatment is in an outpatient office of a dietician, therapist, primary care physician and psychiatrist.
    b. The professional determines the frequency of sessions.
    c. The person with the eating disorder will be held accountable for their behaviors that they are engaging in and if they are unable to lessen the symptoms, they may need a higher level of care.
    d. The dancer with an eating disorder at this level of care may be put on a contract for a certain amount of hours of dancing per week. The contract would be based on whether the person is on weight gain. The person may also be taken out of dance until the increase in weight and/or there is a cessation of eating disorder behaviors.

2. Intensive Outpatient Therapy (IOP)

   The IOP provides more structure than is available in an outpatient setting, as well as offering meal and group support. IOP is usually 3-4 hours per day and 3-5 days per week, depending on the program. The person in IOP may still be engaged in outside activities such as work, school, and dance, if approved by the treatment team. The IOP gives meal support as well as group and individual therapy. The dancer continues to see their outpatient team as additional support. As always, good communication is encouraged between the outpatient providers and whatever level of care the dancer is in. This helps with the eventual transition back to the outpatient provider after successful completion of other levels of treatment. You will need to sign a release for the communication to take place. If the dancer is a minor, the dancer and the parent need to sign the consent form. This is applicable to any level of care. To participate in the IOP level of care, the following criteria must be met:

   a. The person is medically stable. This means that labs and EKG are within the normal range.

   b. The person is able to participate in social, vocational, school and work situations.

   c. The eating disorder symptoms are causing an issue in the person's life, but they can still function in life activities such as school, work and dance if approved by the treatment team.

The IOP is just an additional support for someone who needs more support than outpatient treatment.

3. Partial Hospitalization Program (PHP)
The partial hospitalization program is like an elevator in treatment. It can be used as a place to see if the symptoms can be contained before needing a higher level of care, or it can be used as a step down when a person is leaving residential treatment. The PHP level of care is usually 5-7 days per week and 6-11 hours per day, depending on the facility.

Partial hospitalization is usually held in an office building where they have group rooms, individual offices and a kitchen for the clients to eat their meals. The number of days per week and the hours depend on the program that you choose to attend.

The dancer won't have the ability to dance at this level of care; although, there may come a time when the treatment team begins to look at when the dancer is able to return to dance and for how many hours. Many times, dance can be a motivation for recovery.

In PHP, the dancer will have several groups per day as well as meals and individual sessions with the therapist, dietician and psychiatrist. The program is structured to help the person begin to structure meal times. Be sure there is a family support group as part of the program, as it can be educational for loved ones to help support the person in treatment through this difficult process.

It is important that the PHP you choose has different styles of eating throughout the week. For example, eating styles may include some days where a chef prepares meals; one day they go out to eat at a restaurant; another day they cook with the dietician; other days they bring their own meals. All these varieties of meals are important to break the fear and rules of the eating disorder.

The treatment team works with the dancer to identify the rules and rituals around their eating disorder and begin to break them one by one. In PHP, the dancer is given step down days to begin to test their independence with regards to their ability to be symptom free outside of treatment. Titration of treatment from the number of days attending to the level of treatment is key in the recovery process.

The following are criteria for why someone may need PHP level of care:

a. The person is medically stable, but may have some medical complications from the eating disorder.

b. The eating disorder impairs the person's ability to be able to engage in work, school or any other vocational activity.

c. The person continues to engage in eating disorder behavior on a daily basis and needs the help and structure of the PHP for containment.

4. Residential Treatment Center (RTC)
   A residential treatment center (or residential treatment) is a 24-hour live-in facility, usually in a house/home setting in a residential neighborhood. It is a level of care where the dancer can begin to have relief from the symptoms of the eating disorder and begin to explore the underlying reasons for the behaviors. Remember, it is not about the food! Food and behaviors around food have become the ways for the dancer to express how she is feeling. It is about the underlying reasons and not the food.

For a dancer, it is important that the facility you choose also deals with exercise addiction, even if this is not a specific issue you are dealing with. With such a program, the dancer who wants to return to dance will be able to do some form of exercise during treatment if they are eating their food. A facility that deals with exercise addiction also wants the dancer to be able to participate in physical activity that they will want to continue with once they complete treatment. In addition, the programs often allow the dancer to eventually incorporate yoga and circuit strength training to help them get strong and aid them in returning to the dance studio. There are some programs that don't allow any exercise, so be sure that you are familiar with options.

Residential treatment allows the dancer to learn to eat again, multiple times per day, and recognize that their weight won't get out of control. Trusting the treatment team is a key element and that is especially true with weight gain. The dancer sets an initial weight goal with the dietician. This goal may not be the weight they may actually need to gain, but it is a start. They are put on a meal plan that is individualized for the dancer and have the opportunity to choose some of their meals and snacks, depending on the facility. The staff monitors each person after meals and snacks to make sure they are not purging. Families participate in treatment to learn how to support the dancer on their journey to recovery. If the dancer is living with you when they leave residential treatment, you will want to learn how to be supportive. For family members and friends, it can be like walking through a minefield of grenades. You have to understand what is going to be upsetting to your loved one and develop skills that allow you to approach the subject or communicate in the best way.

Eating disorders are disorders of communication and if the client can learn to identify their feelings and communicate their needs, it will really be a tool they can use on the path to health.

Reasons for Residential Treatment:
a. The person is not so medically compromised and therefore does not require an inpatient setting.
b. Eating disorder behaviors cannot be contained in a PHP or IOP level of care and require 24-hour per day supervision to stop the behaviors.

5. Inpatient Setting
The inpatient setting is in a hospital and offers the medical services that are not available at

residential treatment. Some of the reasons a person may end up in inpatient are: their electrolytes are not in balance or, there is a problem with the cardiovascular function or, they need weight restoration with nutritional care.

In addition, if a person is unable to contract for safety with regard to suicidality, then they will also be hospitalized due to their inability to be safe. Sometimes the eating disorder can make a person anxious and depressed, which can cause suicidal thoughts.

Most inpatient settings are temporary and the person will be transferred to residential treatment after medical stabilization has occurred.

Reasons for Inpatient Care:
a. Suicidal ideation leaves the person unable to make a contract to keep themselves safe.
b. Vital signs are not stable.
c. Medical problems and acute health risk.
d. Increase in the use of eating disorder symptoms.

The goal of treatment is to stabilize the person with the eating disorder, decrease the use of symptoms and explore the purpose the eating disorder has served for this person.

Clients can reach full recovery through outpatient therapy. If the dancer is being seen in outpatient, then they need to see a therapist 1-2 times per week, the dietician at least one time per week, and the primary care physician and psychiatrist on an as needed basis prescribed by the doctors.

The coordination of care is very important in this level, as the client is very vulnerable due to minimal containment. The team needs to be sure that they are delivering a consistent message. Be sure that all consents are signed.

Sometimes dancers have to stop dancing until they agree to gain weight. The return to dance is very gradual and is definitely dependent on the ability to maintain the weight goal.

It is also important that the teacher and/or choreographer are aware of the medical necessity to stop dance for a period of time. The teacher and choreographer can also be very helpful to the team if they are willing to coordinate with the therapist and dietician. Be sure that they are asked to be included and that a release is signed so they can provide information to the treatment team.

If a dancer is seeing a therapist in an outpatient setting and they are struggling to stop behaviors, but continue to dance, a contract may be needed so the client understands what is expected of them in order to continue to dance. Here is an example of the contract that can be used between the dancer and a therapist. If the dancer is a minor, the parents/guardian should be aware of the contract and also sign the agreement. This contract can also help establish parameters for the dancer while in outpatient therapy. Following is a sample contract and different points will be applicable to different clients.

I _____agree to the following...

1. I will follow my meal plan, which is set by the dietician. If I am unable to follow the meal plan and I lose weight, I will not be able to continue to dance and may need a higher level of care.

2. I will reach out for help if I am having a hard time. I recognize that this is part of the recovery process and will be open and honest. I can contact the following people for support and feel comfortable reaching out to them. (This list can be anyone who the person actually thinks they will reach out to in the moment. Below are some suggestions.)
   a. Friend from treatment
   b. Dietician
   c. Therapist
   d. Mom
   e. Sister or brother

3. I will not attend dance class until I have reached my weight goal and have maintained it for _____ period of time. If I am unable to gain weight in outpatient care, I understand that I will need a higher level of care.

4. I agree to not water load or use anything to manipulate my weight before my appointment with the dietician. If I am not being honest about my weight, I will not be able to continue to dance and may need a higher level of care.

5. I recognize that the above is to help me on the road to recovery. I know that I need others to help me fight my eating disorder until I feel stronger and more able to fight it on my own.

Signed and Dated By the Following:

Client_____

Parent _____

Therapist_____

Dietician_____


## Understanding and Navigating Insurance for You or Your Loved One

The duration of treatment is determined by your insurance coverage and limits. Be sure that you know what the insurance out-of-pocket deductible and stop loss payment is for your policy. It is also important to determine if a therapist, or treatment provider, or treatment center is on your insurance plan, or if they are out-of-network. You can still use treatment providers who are out-of-network, but you may have to pay up front and then be reimbursed after you submit the claim. Your insurance will tell you the percentage they pay for out-of-network benefits, but what they may not tell you is that they pay what they feel is reasonable and customary.

For example, you may pay your therapist $175.00 and insurance reimburses you 50% for out-of-network benefits. They may believe that the reasonable and customary amount is $100 per session so they only pay $50.00 instead of $87.50.

Call your insurance provider to get as much information as possible before you start the search for a therapist or treatment. Many eating disorder therapists do not take insurance and will expect payment at the time of services. A good way to find treatment professionals is through edreferral.com (see Chapter 10, Resources for Dancers). On this website, you can look up treatment by zip code. It gives various information about treatment professionals such as: If they accept insurance; If they slide their pay scale; Level of experience in treating eating disorders. It also tells you if they specialize in a certain population—such as dancers.

Other issues that can impact the length of treatment are the duration and intensity of the eating disorder. The sooner the eating disorder is discovered and treatment begins, the better the chance of recovery. But it also depends on other factors. For example, the person may start out in outpatient seeing their team one time per week, or they might begin in a higher level of care where the treatment is more intense due the length of time per day they are in therapy.

# The Fork in the Road...
# Choosing the Path to Recovery

There are many treatment options for the dancer with an eating disorder. Do your research so you can choose the level of care that is necessary, as well as carefully look into the treatment provider and their reputation. The relationship between the therapist and the dancer is such a key element in the recovery process.

Many clients are not ready to gain the weight or to get better if it means completely giving up their eating disorder. Hopefully they have a relationship with a person that they trust and whom they believe can help them in the recovery process. You want the relationship they have with the therapist or treatment team to be more important to the dancer than the relationship with the eating disorder. It takes some time to develop and trust the treatment team or therapist. Somewhere in the dancer with an eating disorder, she has lost trust with herself, her body and others; so developing trust with someone new takes some time. The recovery process is long and requires help from trained experts and support from loved ones, but it will put you, or a loved one on the path to living a healthy life.

# DEAR MOM AND DAD

"I watched my daughter as she began her diet to lose a few pounds. I didn't realize that she would end up in a treatment center for eating disorders."

—Laurie,
a mother of a young dancer

ARENTS PLAY A crucial role in the development of a dancer. As a parent, not only are you the one that's often driving your child to and from the dance studio, conventions, auditions and competitions, but also working to ensure you have a happy and healthy child as they pursue their dream. You may not know the dance world, but it's your job to educate yourself. Unfortunately, eating disorders are often a part of a dancer's life but education is the first step to prevention.

## The Early Role of the Dancer's Parent

When a child is born, a manual is not given to parents to show them how to guide their innocent being through life and accomplish their goals. Many parents have hopes, dreams and expectations about who their child will become. Maybe this beautiful baby will become a teacher, a businessman or woman, or maybe he or she will be the next president. Most parents hope that the child has opportunities that perhaps they never had themselves. One of the most important things you can do as a parent is to support your child in whatever they choose to do, including being a dancer.

When a young child signs up for a dance class, it's just like soccer, baseball, and swimming or piano; it starts off as a recreational sport that allows socialization as well as exercise. For some, all it will ever be is something fun to do after school or on Saturdays. For others, they will eventually discover that they excel at the activity and become more involved. This is the point where it's especially important for parents to be supportive of the child. It's also the moment to recognize the commitment of both time and money for whatever activity there may be, as well as potential problems or risks associated with the activity. In dance, it is important for parents to understand that eating disorders are closely associated with dancers. That doesn't mean all dancers develop an eating disorder, but parents should know the warning signs so they won't be blindsided.

What are some warning signs that my child is developing an eating disorder?

There are very specific signs to look for when a child is developing an eating disorder. Many dancers diet, but you want to pay close attention to the child's inability to stop obsessing about food, calories and weight. Eating disorders are not a choice that someone makes.

Here are some signs your child may be struggling with an eating disorder:

- Your young dancer has begun to isolate and spends more time alone and in her room when not at the studio.

- She goes to the bathroom a lot after meals, or maybe she skips meals with the family because she "already ate."

- Food is disappearing from the pantry.

- You notice she is losing weight, but she says she needs to lose a few pounds for the upcoming performance.

- She wears baggy clothes all the time to hide her recent weight loss.

More information about warning signs and prevention is available in Chapter 4 (Warning Signs and the Prevention of Eating Disorders for Dancers).

## How can I be an active parent?

At some point, perhaps at a summer program or perhaps earlier, a young dancer experiences themselves in relationship to many other dancers. They begin to compare their technique, as well as their bodies, to others. Usually around the time that a dancer begins going to the summer intensives is about the time that they are entering puberty. This can be a difficult time for a dancer, because there are pressures to have a certain type of body, depending on the style of dance. It's also the time when eating disorders and problems with depression and self-esteem can begin. Pressure may come from the teacher, the choreographer, peers, or possibly the dancer themselves. Some dancers will not be affected by negative comments from a teacher or choreographer, but someone with the predisposition for an eating disorder or depression may begin to focus on their body if negative comments are made.

Individuals with eating disorders usually have very low self-esteem. You can help your young dancer by focusing on the positives of her passion for dance. When a dancer feels proud of their talent and what they can do with the body, it helps them not only in dance, but hopefully not to develop an eating disorder.

As a parent, make an effort to find out what is being said to your dancer. A dance teacher's negative comment can spark a desire to lose weight. Not everyone who hears a negative comment about their body in dance class is going to develop an eating disorder. But some will, which is why awareness of what is being verbalized to dancers is important. You want to guide your child toward the best classes and care possible. At each step in this process, check to be sure that the dancer is being given the proper instruction. This includes making certain that teachers are not putting an emphasis on the size of the body.

Be aware and observant of the beliefs of the teacher around this area. Some teachers weigh students or post a "fat" list. This is unacceptable. Ensure that your dancer can get an education in dance without being subjected to abusive practices about weight or body. Make it a priority to be aware of your child's dance environment, and only choose instructors who help your child love and respect themselves as they learn. If you're concerned that a teacher is putting undue pressure on body size, have an open discussion with the instructor about your concerns.

If you believe your child is hearing negative comments about their body, you can take the following actions:

- Watch the class with the teacher who is making the comments. Many studios have window walls or closed-circuit TVs, so it shouldn't be a problem to check in.

- If the teacher makes negative comments about your child, or other children in the class, approach the teacher with your concerns about the comments. The teacher may be unaware of how the child perceives what they say.

- Have a conversation to reinforce positive body image in your child. Talk about how beautiful it is for their body to be able to dance and move the way it does, to music.

- Remind the student that it takes food to fuel our bodies, and how important that is when you're dancing so much.

## How do I know my child is enrolled at the right school?

For the parent of a dancer, it is essential that your child study dance at a reputable studio. This doesn't always mean the largest studio, but it does mean that the instructors are well-trained and good teachers. Someone can be an excellent dancer but they may not be a good teacher, so try to rely more on an individual's ability as a teacher and their relationship with their students, rather than simply their credits.

Be sure and consider what type of dance is taught at the studio; for example, is it strictly a ballet studio, or are all forms of dance taught? Ballet is the foundation of dance, so finding a studio where ballet is required of all dancers is important, especially if your child wants to pursue dance as a serious hobby or career. From ballet, other forms of dance can be expanded upon. A tap, jazz, contemporary, or musical theatre dancer needs ballet in order to improve technique in other forms of dance. For example, it is key for a tap dancer to be able to turn and spot; and this is a technique that is taught in ballet. The goal is to have a well-rounded dancer who can use the technique from ballet in all areas of dance.

In a dance studio where ballet is the focus, the emphasis is much different. The dancer may be required to take at least two ballet classes per week to start, and then progress as the levels increase. From there, they advance through the levels of ballet as their technique improves. Dancers should also be given opportunities to study at different summer intensives. These summer intensives can be facilitated through a ballet company such as the American Ballet Theatre, the Miami City Ballet, the San Francisco Ballet, the Houston Ballet, the Boston Ballet, or other companies; or it can be summer intensive offered through a college or school.

Find out who will be teaching at the summer programs. Most programs bring on reputable teachers and choreographers for the summer. If you are sending your child away for a six-week program, do the research. Know where they'll be housed and how they'll be supervised. This has the potential to be a wonderful growth experience for a young dancer filled with hope and dreams, but it can also be a dangerous situation if your child is suffering from an eating disorder. As a parent, be sure all your questions are answered. If they aren't, don't be afraid to speak up and ask.

## How do we deal with auditions?

The career of a dancer is filled with auditions and rejections, but hopefully the dancer, whether professional or student learns something from each experience. Help your young dancer gain an understanding of the audition process; then help them accept that if they are not selected for a particular program, they have to be able to take a correction and apply it to the next audition. Allowing this to be a positive learning experience without affecting their self-esteem is really crucial.

An audition for a summer program in a big city is an experience for the young dancer that can be educational and stressful at the same time. In the dancer's home studio, they compare themselves to the other dancers and know how they measure up—but at the audition, they have the experience of meeting dancers from other areas and taking classes from new teachers, which can be both intimidating and very exciting. Be sure and communicate with your child about all aspects of their experience, including the audition process.

Here are some ways to help a child cope with the pressure of a successful audition, both before and after:

- Before the audition, the student should understand the process of the audition. Hopefully the teacher has explained this to the dancer. If not, as a parent ask as many questions as you can to help both you and your child to gain an understanding of the process.

- Help your child know if they want to pursue dancing, this is just one of many auditions in their life. They should do their best and be proud of what they can do.

- In the audition, it helps your child's self-esteem and performance if they don't compare themselves to other dancers, but instead stay self-focused.

- Remind your dancer to be a good sport and wish others well. If their peer is selected after the audition, remind them to offer congratulations.

- If your child is selected, congratulate them and let them know how proud you are. If they are not selected, go ahead and let them know how proud you are and that there will be other auditions. Difficult as it can be, a young dancer must learn they will find the program best suited for their style of dance.

## All of my daughter's friends are on diets. What should I tell my dancer about food and nutrition?

A dancer can end up spending more time with their dance teacher than they do at home, especially if pursuing a professional career. As a parent, you matter. Your child looks to you for guidance and reassurance that what they are doing is correct. Rather than assume the only adult your young dancer listens to is their teacher, take an active role by actually talking about good nutrition.

A dancer's body is important because it's the instrument that allows them to tell a story. That's why it's so crucial the dancer understands essential nutrition and recognizes that food is the fuel the body needs to be able to dance. A young dancer who understands the need for food to nourish the body and who has a healthy self-esteem is less likely to be impacted by negative comments from others. When you develop dancers who feel good about themselves, it allows them to enjoy the art form of dance. It also permits them to feel the music and not be stuck in their head about whether or not they did the correct step. While it's important that dancers have the ability to learn choreography, it is more important they feel the music, otherwise, we would have robots for dancers who are always in their head and concerned about what others think of them, rather than expressive dancers who are nourished both physically and creatively.

Keep in mind:

- Don't restrict your child to only low-calorie foods.

- Be sure your child always has nutritious snacks in their dance bag in case they're hungry between classes. (If you are unsure of what good nutrition is, seek advice from a registered dietician and see additional information in Chapter 6, The Balanced Barre: Balancing Nutrition without Obsessing Over Calories).

- Don't criticize your body in front of your child. Be a positive role model in your dancer's life by accepting your body and eating regular meals.

- Consider taking scales out of your house so the dancer isn't weighing in every day.

- Remind your child that food is fuel, not a reward.

Emphasize the importance of who your child is as a person rather than the size of their body. Good self-esteem and confidence in self allow the dancer to take pride in their abilities. This confidence will get them far in their life as a dancer or in any career they choose. If they're happy in their life and doing what they love, food will not have the power in their life. If your young dancer understands this, then they are on the right track.

# Are dance competitions bad for my child?

Life is filled with competition, and so is dance. These days, many dancers begin competing at a young age. There are competitions for dance everywhere. Some are associated with dance conventions, and others are competitions only.

For the average dancer, competitions can be a great experience. But for someone with an eating disorder, this competitiveness can fuel their eating disorder as they strive for perfection in dance as well as in their body. It can become a competition about body size, as well as dance. A dancer needs to be in a healthy place in recovery in order to compete in the dance world. They must follow their meal plan and recognize there is no such thing as perfection. Instead, they can strive to be the best dancer they can be.

Deciding whether participation in a competition team is going to further the dancer's career is an important determination. Competition is helpful for dancers who have no other way to perform. It can also be a way to see how you measure up against other dancers from other areas. Looking at the sensitivity of the dancer is key. If a dancer has a low self- esteem and is very sensitive, competition may not be the right avenue. Although most competitions give positive feedback to dancers, it can be difficult for those who don't win.

As a parent, preparing students for competition includes education about the process and what to expect. Reassure your dancer that it's about the experience and not the award. Competing shouldn't be seen as the end goal or ultimate measure of success. Dance, similar to recovery, is about the process and not the end result. If the dancer understands this concept, then they can feel less disappointed if they do not win at the first competition. Instead they can use the critiques to improve their skill and continue to progress. Competition can be educational for a dancer if it is kept in the right perspective.

The competition can be a part of the dancer's life, but there must be good education. Dance is not just about preparing for the next competition, but should also focus on technique and the ability to dance to the music. There is more to dance than performance. The dancer who is able to focus on the music and stay in touch with physical technique is already ahead in eating disorder prevention or recovery because they're focusing on the process and not the end result.

You can help your dancer learn how to be a good sport in the arena of competition. Teachers and parents have an influential role here, much like teaching your children manners as a young child. There is the etiquette of being polite to other dance groups. It can be as simple as saying "great job" to another group or being respectful of the space in the dressing rooms. Some competitions facilitate and recognize this etiquette by giving awards for the group who has the best sportsmanship backstage.

Competitions are a good place for dancers to learn from the critiques of other professionals. These critiques are usually ones they've heard many times from their own teacher, but hearing it from someone else sometimes helps the dancers to apply the correction.

DEAR MOM AND DAD

As with any critique, the ability to respond to feedback constructively and from a place of positive self-esteem helps the dancer to improve their dance abilities, rather than resort to disordered eating due to feelings of not being not good enough.

A dancer can also learn a lot from watching other dancers perform outside of their regular studio. It provides perspective from somewhere other than the place they study. What's more, they're exposed to other dancers, teachers and choreographers from all over the country. Help your dancer to learn from observation rather than compare their bodies to other dancers by having them observe the other dancers. Have them tell you the dances they enjoyed and why. What was it about the dancers that caught their eye? This helps them to see what other dancers are doing. It will also give you an idea of what they are seeing in the performance. If they talk about the other dancer's body, it could be a warning sign, but also an opportunity for conversation and growth.

It is important for parents to understand that some dancers are not ready to compete. You shouldn't force a child to continue to participate in dance or in competitions when they don't have the interest. Just as important is that a child understands commitment. Life is filled with commitments, not just in dance. If a dancer decides they don't want to dance anymore, take time to hear and listen to them, but also explain the importance of commitment. If a dancer is committed to a team through the end of the year, then encourage them to finish. At that point, they can make the decision to continue to be a part of the team, or if they even want to dance at all.

## How can I avoid being a "stage mom"?

Having a stage mom or dad can be difficult for a dancer. Ask yourself, am I pushing my child to dance for my own personal reasons? Many stage parents live vicariously through their children, so it's an important question to answer with honesty. The dancer needs to enjoy dance and have it be their choice to attend class.

Some dancers feel the pressure to follow their parents' dream. They dance because they think this is what their mom or dad wants them to do. Maybe the mom never got to dance, so she wants to offer that opportunity to her daughter. That is wonderful if the daughter wants it for herself, but if she is doing it to please someone other than herself, the end result can be problematic.

If your child does not get a certain part or is not in the front row, trust the teacher or choreographer with their decision. After all, you chose this teacher so you must trust them. Do not let your ego drive your discussions about your child. When you are constantly asking questions about why your child didn't get a certain part or put in certain place in the dance, it can become very frustrating to the teacher and embarrassing to your child.

# What if my child wants to quit dancing?

Many times a discouraged student may not truly want to quit dance or the team, so take care to talk and get to really understand what is going on with the dancer.

Are they stressed with school? If a student is struggling with school, then look at ways they can have more time to complete homework. Maybe they need help with time management. As the parent, you may need to talk to the dance teacher about your concerns and see if there are classes your dancer is not required to attend. Perhaps fewer classes would help the dancer to feel less stressed. The dancer may need a little more time for projects at school, and with a few adjustments this can be accommodated, helping them to feel better about both school and dance. Be aware of the pressures and concerns of your dancer without being intrusive, and be ready to offer solutions.

Stress can be a contributing factor in the development of an eating disorder. Often, someone who develops an eating disorder is always concerned about pleasing others, many times at the expense of themselves. The dancer may be fearful of disappointing a teacher or their parents. Openly communicate your desire to help them, and respond positively when they open up to you.

The balance of commitment to dance, along with making sure the stress is reduced, is a fine line in the dancer's life. Once again, open dialogue and communication is so important in this process. As a parent you can ask your child, "How can I be supportive?" You may be surprised that many children are able to give very direct feedback to this question. Simply asking helps them understand that their health is valuable and they can come to you for support.

The most important thing is to listen to your dancer, see what their concerns are, and why they want to stop dancing. Be empathetic, because they want to be heard. If there's a specific concern such as school, try to reduce the dance classes (if possible) to allow the child to have time to complete assignments.

Perhaps they've started puberty and feel uncomfortable in their dance clothes? Pay attention to how they relate to their body and clothing, as so much time is spent looking in the mirror and watching their body move. When a young dancer's body begins to mature and develop, it can be devastating. It could be the reason behind the desire to quit dance. If your child is struggling with body image, take time to explain the natural evolution of our bodies, and that it is normal for the body to change. The more you can normalize this process for the child hopefully the less they'll be focused on the process. Remember, they are looking to you to be their role model and to guide them through difficult times.

## How can my dancer be a good student, participate in other activities and have friends and relationships outside of dance?

There are dancers who participate in activities at school such as cheerleading, dance team, drill team, band, track and other sports. This can cause stress for the dancer because there can be conflicts at times, leaving them to choose one activity over another. It's also a concern because other activities could cause injuries that affect the ability to dance. If a dancer is able to participate in dance and another activity at school, there is little free time because time not spent at school is spent in the dance studio.

There are students who are very dedicated to dance but who also find ways to balance their life with other activities. They are involved in clubs at school, cheerleading and track. They spend many hours at the dance studio but also have time to participate in school activities. This is important, especially for a dancer who enjoys dance, but is not sure it's the path to choose as a profession.

To help your dancer balance school with dance, make sure their dance schedule allows them enough time to complete homework. Maybe they can be taken out of physical education, which could provide a study period at school to complete their homework. If they're taking many dance classes per week, you might see if the dance teacher can sign a form for the school to allow dance to count toward the physical education requirement. You can also talk to the school about independent study and explore various options.

To help your dancer balance relationships with dance, you can encourage them to have relationships outside of the studio. Your dancer should have diverse friends, including friends who are not from the dance world. Encouraging dancers to make time to spend with these friends is also important. Maybe attending a school football game or going to the movies with them would be a great start. Keeping your dancer's life as balanced as possible, without putting undo stress on them to do yet one more thing, can help them achieve balance in areas related to food and body image as well. Time with friends should be fun and enjoyable, not something that has to be accomplished "because my mom or dad want me to."

To help your dancer balance other activities with dance, offer them assistance with managing their calendar. They may have difficulties maneuvering through the challenges of scheduling different activities and become easily overwhelmed.

When a dancer wants to pursue other activities, it's very important that you support them. Don't discourage other pursuits because you want them to be a dancer. If the dancer is meant to dance, they'll find the road back to dancing. Allowing space for other activities may help them discover that dance really is what they are passionate about, while enabling them to find it out for themselves.

## My daughter wants to skip college and pursue a professional dance career. Should I support this?

Today there are so many colleges that specialize in dance. A dancer can attend a college that is associated with a dance program and needn't give up either dance or a college degree. An example of this is Fordham University and Ailey School in New York City. Students have the opportunity to study dance at the Ailey School while earning a BFA degree from Fordham University. Dominican University of California is another similar program, where dancers combine education and an artistic program associated with Alonzo King's LINES in San Francisco.

In addition, there are specific programs to prepare dancers and singers for a career in musical theatre. The University of Cincinnati, University of Michigan, State University of New York Purchase, Oklahoma City University, University of North Carolina School of the Arts, and University of California at Irvine are a few of the top contenders for the department of musical theatre. It's a good idea for the dancer to have a minor in another subject, because a dancer's career can be cut short by an injury. Having additional skills to fall back on can be very helpful.

## I have tried to be the best parent possible. How can I best support my child but not let on that I think there may be an eating disorder issue?

Ask questions. You can start by saying to your child that you noticed she is eating less, and ask if everything is all right. The dancer may not answer you, but now they know you are aware and noticing the different behaviors. So you don't put them on the defense, be mindful that a combination of curiosity and empathy makes the best recipe for success when approaching someone. Also, asking the dance teacher if they've noticed anything different while at the studio can be helpful.

When a dancer wants to pursue other activities, it's very important that you support them. Don't discourage other pursuits because you want them to be a dancer.

If the problem persists and weight loss continues, it may be necessary to seek treatment for the eating disorder. The sooner the problem is addressed, the better prognosis for treatment. If you see any of the signs mentioned, it's a good idea to seek professional advice. The therapist or dietician will advise you on a treatment plan. Make sure you see a therapist with a specialization in eating disorders. It is imperative that the dancer connects with the therapist also. You may have to interview several therapists until the dancer feels comfortable. Please refer to Chapter 10 (Resources for Dancers), which lists resources for eating disorder treatment. You can also find organizations that are supportive of parents of a child with an eating disorder.

The therapist will most likely refer the dancer to a registered dietician who also specializes in eating disorders. The dietician and the therapist should work together on the treatment for the dancer. The dietician gives the dancer a meal plan to follow, and the dancer should be weighed with their back to the scale to prevent them from obsessing about their weight.

In some cases, your dancer may not be able to continue to dance until receiving treatment for the eating disorder. This is a possible and hopeful scenario, and many times it can be a motivating factor for them to become well. Some therapists work with a registered dietician, and together they provide a contract for the dancer so they are aware of what has to be done in order to return to dance. The dancer should also be seeing a medical doctor who gives them the medical clearance to return to dance. See Chapter 8 (Treatment Options for the Dancer) for more information about the different treatments available for dancers.

An eating disorder can develop for a multitude of reasons. Just because your child wants to be a dancer doesn't mean that they will develop an eating disorder. But if they do, you can be a big help by educating yourself, your dancer and the teacher. Helping means taking steps to help your child recover.

# RESOURCES FOR DANCERS

THE FOLLOWING NATIONAL organizations offer referral lists for therapists, doctors, dieticians and other treatment options for the dancer with an eating disorder.

Be sure that the professional specializes in the treatment of eating disorders. A certification from the IAEDP (listed below) indicates someone has worked with eating disorders for a designated period of time and is trained in the field of eating disorders.

AED, Academy for Eating Disorders. *aedweb.org*

ANAD, National Association of Anorexia Nervosa and Associated Disorders, *anad.org*

F.E.A.S.T., Families Empowered & Supporting Treatment of Eating Disorders, *feast-ed.org*

IAEDP, International Association of Eating Disorders Professionals, *iaedp.com*

NEDA, National Eating Disorders Association, *nationaleatingdisorders.org*

OA, Overeaters Anonymous, *oa.org*

## Additional Organizations:

The Academy of Nutrition and Dietetics (*eatright.org*) provides information on eating disorders as well as referrals for dieticians who treat eating disorders.

IADMS, International Association for Dance Medicine & Science, *iadms.org*

University of Wisconsin, Dancers Clinic, *uwhealth.org*

Cedars-Sinai/USC Glorya Kaufman Dance Medicine Center, *cedars-sinai.edu*

*Eatingdisordersblogs.com* Provides up-to-date information, thoughts and ideas on eating disorders and related topics such as body image, exercise addiction, research, education and families.

EDReferral (Eating Disorder Referral and Information Center) is a website (*EDReferral.com*) where you can find free support groups, interventionists, doctors, therapists and dieticians in the United States and Canada. EDReferral also has numerous topics on eating disorders to help you get the information you need.

## Publications:

*Dance Magazine* (*dancemagazine.com*) publishes an annual college guide in August with more than 600 entries, providing information about the college/ university, their specialty, how many students are in the dance program and much more. Print and online guides available.

*Dance Spirit Magazine* (*dancespirit.com*) has many great articles on nutrition and eating disorders for dancers.

Gürze Books, LLC (*gurzebooks.com*) has been publishing trade books on eating disorders since 1980 and has links to online purchasing.

# ACKNOWLEDGEMENTS

THANK YOU TO all my students and clients throughout the years. You gave me the opportunity to learn from you along my journey. Each person has made an impact on my life, and I am blessed to know such wonderful people.

I want to acknowledge my mother, Nellie Lou "Skipper" Downie Smith. She had a dance studio for 55 years in Ohio, was an inspiration to many of her students, and dedicated time to working with the physically challenged. She was featured on the back cover of *Dance Magazine* in November 1975. She moved to Maui in 1998 where she continued to spread her love of dance with the young dancers on Maui. I was dancing with her before I was born. We shared our love of dance for many years together. She also supported me in my struggle through years of anorexia and subsequent recovery to become the person I am today.

Thank you to Karen Decker, Jacque Mular, Tina DePizzo and Brooke Glazer, all registered dieticians who specialize in eating disorders and helped with Chapter 6 (*The Balanced Barre: Balancing Nutrition without Obsessing Over Calories*). They each provided invaluable information regarding meals, snacks and caloric values.

Thank you to all the dancers who took time out of your busy lives and allowed me to interview you. Each of your stories is valuable and an integral part of the book.

Thank you Gürze Books for referring me to Spencer Smith, who referred me to Anna Mantzaris. Thank you Anna for encouraging me to complete the project. I appreciate the time and energy you put into helping me with the book. Thank you Angela Frucci for making my book ready for publication.

Thank you Saroyan Humphrey for the beautiful cover page design and layout of the book.

Kyla Buckingham was an inspiration in the beginning of my project. I appreciate your time, energy and belief in *TuTu Thin*.

Thank you Carolyn Costin for being my mentor for the past 15 years. You made me the therapist I am today. I am honored you wrote the foreword for my book.

Thank you to my husband, Dean Anthony Theodore, who supports me in all my projects. You are always there for me and I am so happy we are partners for life.

To my family and friends who have loved and supported me throughout my life.  I am blessed to have such great people for a support system.

Lastly, I thank my eating disorder. Without having the opportunity to recover, I would not be the person I am today.

BIO

DAWN THEODORE, MA, MFT, CEDS, is a leader in the treatment of eating disorders. She brings to her practice the insights of a teacher, studio owner and dancer who recovered from anorexia nervosa. She is currently the Director of Day Treatment Services for Monte Nido & Affiliates. She also has a private therapy practice in Calabasas and Brentwood, California.

*HealthZone with Amy Hendel* and *Recovery Talk Network* showcased her groundbreaking contribution to the treatment of eating disorders. Pepperdine University and California State University, Dominguez Hills, invited her to speak on this affliction affecting so many women (and men, too). "Starving Secrets," a *Lifetime Channel* documentary about eating disorders, invited her to share her insights on eating disorders.

She wrote the chapter "Fit or Fanatic" (with Carolyn Costin in 1997) in her rewrite of *Your Dieting Daughter*, released in 2013. Dawn also contributed to *The Recovery Journal*, shedding light on the relationship between eating disorders and the widespread use of crystal meth.

Dawn owned and operated a dance studio in Calabasas for twenty-five years. Before opening her studio, Dawn lived in New York City where she worked with the legendary Henry LeTang, appearing in his productions and teaching in his studio. Dawn is the co-owner of Cross Pointe Dance, a Master Class series and performance opportunity for young dancers. She has been featured in many commercials and TV shows.